SUPREMACY

AND

PEACE

By

CHARLES C. HILLIARD

THE NORTH RIVER PRESS

NEW YORK · 1956

COPYRIGHT, 1956, BY
CHARLES C. HILLIARD

PRINTED IN THE UNITED STATES OF AMERICA

Library of Congress Catalog Card No. 56-8435

TO
PROVIDENCE
AND
PATRIOTS

CONTENTS

		PAGE
Preface		ix

PART I

The Nature of the Argument

CHAPTER

| 1. | The Restless Search for Truth | 1 |
| 2. | Thought | 11 |

PART II

Principle and Power

3.	The General Theory of Benevolent Supremacy	37
4.	The Scheme and Pattern of Reality	46
5.	Dialectical Materialism	59
6.	Of Ergs, Dynes and Effort	75
7.	Religion and Politics	91
8.	On Evolving Toward Perfection	106
9.	Law and Order	121

PART III

Politics and Peace

10.	Government Responsive to Benevolent Ideal	139
11.	The Distribution of Wealth	152
12.	Education and Willingness	167
13.	On Nations' Being United	179
14.	Patriotism, Readiness and Action	195
15.	Peace	206

PREFACE

THIS book believes in absolute principle and is highly in favor of the idea that " 'Impossible' is only for the weak and those of little faith . . ."

To begin with, however, a few words about theories, including a definition. One reason for the writing of "Supremacy and Peace" is to carry forward, in the light of criticism and of further experience and thought, some of the ideas set forth in an earlier book of mine, "The Cross, The Sword and The Dollar," published in 1951. Both of these books look for the right answers to questions with which we, as citizens of the American Republic, are faced in our time.

The present volume, as compared with its predecessor, seeks to establish a theory. The mission of this book is to consider the source and nature of sovereign power, to define moral force as well as physical energy and, in the process, to evolve a workable theory of the design and use of such elements in government.

In these pages, theory is taken to mean a proposed explanation of a phenomenon, an explanation of why and how the various elements of a system work together to accomplish one result instead of another. The proposed explanation must be verifiable by observation and experiment, but not necessarily reducible to a mathematical formula. Theories may be so called when they are only arbitrary assumptions, hypotheses without basis in fact, merely unsupported imaginings. This is a pitfall to be avoided carefully, if the development of a theory is to accomplish its aim.

It is sometimes by means of theories that men can be prepared for otherwise overwhelming eventualities, that man can avoid being caught unprepared in the face of actual conditions. Theories, whether they be obscure or obvious, well or poorly tested, can be classed as specialized or as of general application. In any case, the approach to problems by way of theory is, in itself, not only a time-honored practice, but also a natural method by which advancement in human knowledge is made.

It is a surprising fact, indeed almost unbelievable, that there has not been formulated long ago, and confirmed by experiment, a sound and general theory of the political system, a lasting theory of government based explicitly on the principle of human existence, which is also known as the principle of Christianity. Such lack of political development seems, nevertheless, to be the case. Or, at least, I, for one, know of no such theory. In our time, attention has been directed more to an improvement of the framework and the machinery of government than to a better understanding of the character and the formal behavior of the forces which a government brings to bear upon its problems.

In consequence, this book is interested in the formulation, as well as in the proof, of the general theory above mentioned. Thought is an essential part of the considerations. It is also an unfathomed element. Admittedly with some hesitation, then, this volume goes so far as to give an arbitrary meaning to thought itself.

The following pages may be found to contain only an ordinary sequence of ideas on subjects such as the principle of benevolent sovereignty in search of a political party in our country. What they record may amount to that, at least. At most, the argument can be found to contain an old, convincing and powerful philosophy.

C. C. H.

New York, N. Y.
February 1, 1956

Part I

The Nature of the Argument

CHAPTER ONE

The Restless Search for Truth

THE ideal is an inevitable factor in the living of a human life. It is also a factor of unusual importance. It is mixed up somehow with the emotions. Alexander is said to have wept when he thought that there were no more worlds to conquer. And, from early times, the ideal has been likened to a star, or the star has been taken to relate to the ideal and other matters of destiny.

According to the record, the ancients spoke of an association of this kind. At least, Pindar seems to have noticed it—"It is the natal star that ruleth over every deed." Later on, there is Shakespeare's "The fault, dear Brutus, is not in our stars, but in ourselves." And, more recently, we have been advised by no less an authority than Mr. Emerson, the sage of Concord, to "Hitch your wagon to a star." In any case, there is enough evidence to make it sensible to include a more or less definite meaning of the ideal at the beginning of the present inquiry.

From the human's point of view, the ideal is a form of wish. It represents a desire. Formally, and usually, an ideal is taken to be the highest type of excellence, or a final goal. But, as a matter of fact, what anyone desires to accomplish or to possess in the ordinary course of events is by way of becoming an ideal. It is the immediate ideal, as of a given place and moment. It is also an ideal in the sense of either a general idea

1

of perfection, or a mental picture of excellence, in particular. There are, then, an infinite number of ideals, great and lesser, abstract and concrete. And the whole affair is as systematic as can be, in witness of which there is the scheme and pattern of life that surrounds us and of which we are a part.

Not only is the ideal itself important, but the rôle which the ideal plays is also vital. And there is little doubt that many mistakes are, and have been, made in life concerning the intended function of the ideal and of its close relative, the standard of perfection. The abstract ideal, in the form of an absolute standard, is mistaken for the concrete objective, and vice versa. This is an especially significant fact bearing on the problems now ahead of us for consideration. It would be hard to overestimate its importance.

The well-chosen ideal is at the heart of every success. On the other hand, mistakes about the moral rôle of the ideal— of the spiritual ideal, to be more precise in present context— have led not only to varying degrees of personal dissatisfaction, including disappointment and bitterness, but also to eccentric ideologies. They have led, for instance, to Nietzsche's doctrine of the superman, to Tolstoy's retreat from everyday realities, to Spengler's hopelessness regarding the trend of Western culture and civilization and to more than a few social plans of the self-defeating sort. Mistakes about the intended rôle of the ideal have contributed to the political confusions and the strifes of yesterday and of today.

There is many an ideal that is no more fully attainable in the current of daily affairs than is the fixed star that serves to guide the voyager on a true course. But the light of an ideal can be infinitely more far-reaching than the light of any star. Ideals, in the abstract, can be changeless standards of perfection, each truly good ideal of a merit equal to that of every other of the same quality, all springing from the same source, or principle—or, so we can assume initially. As abstractions, ideals are intangibles, which does not mean that their function is useless, but the contrary.

For sake of contrast, compare the ideal with, say, a virtue. A virtue, in its primary meaning, relates particularly to moral excellence. Human choice between right and wrong is implicit. All true virtues, by nature, represent unchanging standards of personal perfection for the human race, whereas a currently accepted ideal may be virtuous or not. Virtues are naturally ideals, but chosen ideals are not always virtuous.

Prudence, justice, fortitude and temperance, faith, hope and charity—virtues classed as cardinal or otherwise—are only generalizations, if you like, when viewed as qualities. So, too, is the quality of the idea of security, and of similar aims, along with the abstract ideal itself. In being put to practical advantage, all generalizations need to be brought to task in terms of familiar circumstances and actual events.

Great causes spring from great ideals but are naturally personalized in great leaders. Likewise, they are connected in thought with particular times and places, and with cherished symbols. Hence, also, the lasting value of the fable and the parable as vehicles of the changeless truth.

It would seem from such preliminary observations that the ideal and the part played by the ideal are, indeed, always more than casually related to the nature of human effort, for or against. That is, after all, the sort of endeavor in which each one of us is engaged.

2.

In New York, just after you cross the Queensboro Bridge from the Borough of Manhattan and enter Long Island City's Bridge Plaza—on the way, for instance, to LaGuardia Airport

—there is to the right, over an entrance to the Eagle Electric Manufacturing Company, an inscription that says:

*"Perfection Is Not
An Accident."*

It is an idea to think about. In fact, it can be not only a reassuring idea, but also one that raises questions. So, actually, it joins forces with the International Business Machines Corporation, and with others who urge us in their household slogans, publications and other means of admonition, to "think."

It is a favorite assertion of philosophers and others that everything around us gives a clue to the meaning of the universe. It appears to be a correct statement of the situation. There is here no desire to belittle in the least, but quite the contrary, the value of information to be deduced from such clues, even if that method of searching for general conclusions is not always the most productive of prompt and useful answers.

In addition to considerations of method, however, there is intended here a due regard for the thoughts and experiences of others, as also for discussion, public and private. There is an immense respect for good teachings, including good example. At the same time, there is for each human being, it would seem, no satisfactory substitute for his own interest in thinking for himself. He might well think for himself, especially in respect to ideas habitually accepted as true, or as untrue, by his contemporaries.

To lapse for a moment into autobiography—it is admitted in advance that, for purposes of background, there will be a few such lapses along the way—I would not like to guess how many odds and ends of information and how many sketchy memoranda on apparently separate and irrelevant subjects I have collected, then put aside for future reference, or thrown away, during the past ten years or so, not to say the last thirty years and more. Perhaps this was because of curiosity to see if they would fall, sooner or later, into a general pattern. They do.

There is one of the older notes, for instance, about the contrast between East and West in the matter of coaling ship at Nagasaki, of all places. It is a good, hill-rimmed harbor, incidentally, but a forlorn spot at first glance, after viewing the region around Yokohama and the beauty of the Inland Sea. The "S/S Empress of Russia" the ship was—in 1916 when coaling at Nagasaki was still done by the sweat of the brow.

Long lines of men and women, I remember, on rope ladders down the side of the big ship, men and women passing up from hand to hand small, fibre baskets shaped somewhat like large rice bowls and filled with lumps of the fuel. No time out for inalienable rights and refreshing pauses, but much apparently cheerful bantering along with the endless-chain routine of the persistent baskets. Sturdy Japanese bodies glistening in the hot summer sun.

Other ways and means of doing a useful job. Other points of view. Other assets and liabilities. Other taboos. Another nation, language and tradition. Geographical differences, and no mistake about that. One world, one world politically? The question did not occur to me.

At that time, the United States had not yet entered World War I. A London darkened against Zeppelin raids was still fresh in mind. The radio and aeroplane, even the automobile, were still infants. Talking pictures were yet to come. Television existed only in the imagination. In the preceding year President Wilson had made his much criticized speech about being "too proud to fight." After the comparatively peaceful times that ushered in the 20th century, the world situation was already becoming almost daily more confused.

In view of a rather casual approach to knowledge through the collection of stray bits of information above mentioned, it was encouraging to me, not to say comforting, recently to run across a quotation from the writings of Count Rumford (1753-1814), born Benjamin Thompson, in Massachusetts, and, as you may also recall, famed for his observations and findings in regard to the nature of heat. Thus, in turn, he was partly responsible also for the theory of the conservation of energy. Said the Count:

> "... a habit of keeping the eyes open to every thing that is going on in the ordinary course of the business of life has oftener led, as it were by accident, or in the playful excursions of the imagination, put into action by contemplating the most common appearances, to useful doubts, and sensible schemes for investigation and improvement, than all the more intense meditations of philosophers, in the hours expressly set apart for study ..."

I hope so—and there is still another reason for liking this comment of the worthy Count.

There is always a reason. In this instance, it is because the comment is made in a good, long sentence, no less, one that requires sustained thought for more than seven to ten words at a time. Incidentally, if you go in for rambling excursions of the kind, Nathaniel Hawthorne has a sentence some 139 words long in his introductory chapter of "The Scarlet Letter."

There is much to be said for "clarity, brevity and exactness." For the military, among others, there are times and places in which it is an essential combination, not that all necessary information can always be condensed safely on one page. But consider the subject of a brief sentence in another setting. The short phrase or the clause may nearly always be adapted to context and the ellipsis practically limits its own use, but the short sentence, for the sake of the short sentence, one after another, becomes monotonous. Monotony and variety, the happy medium and the exception to the rule—already we find relationships which need to be looked into as striking deeper than meets the eye.

3.

In the early 1930s, I was one of the large and admiring public of Arthur Brisbane. In his syndicated column, then appearing in the *Hearst* and other newspapers throughout the country, he put forward over and over again, in various words, the following thought—

> What mankind can imagine, it can do. What
> man can imagine, he can do.

It is an expression of his—perhaps oversimplified in the above language—that has had an influence on the eventual writing of this book. By intuition, it is possible to feel that there is truth contained in the idea. But, by personal experience, we know that man can imagine opposites which contradict each other, that he can imagine quality and the abstract, as well as quantity and the concrete circumstance. It is all puzzling enough.

The search for truth, a search in the form of argument, or process of proof, needs to be methodical, as a rule, in order to be thorough and reasonably convincing. In an initial chapter of the present kind, however, we can, at least, point separately to a few further subjects, and questions thereon, which concern the argument and which are likely to enter the discussion again and more connectedly at a later time.

For example, there is a subject such as the working pattern of the day-to-day course of events which, for us humans, seems to involve a state of balance, moment by moment, between mutually opposing forces. It is a pattern in which strengths and forces are noticeably set in opposition to each other by the impacts of contradictory ideals and of conflicting ideas.

Is opposition, in itself, then, either good, or bad? Or, is opposition simply a fact which may be turned to either right or wrong purpose?

Leaving right and wrong for future definition, we can safely say, as a beginning, that good is represented by any idea or force which strengthens the trend of affairs toward perfection and that the character of any idea or force contrary thereto is evil. Also, it can be reasoned, without delay, that the force which operates in the direction of perfect existence—that is, the force of good will, or benevolence— must be able always to overcome the adversity of resistance to its progress and, likewise, able to reverse an opposing trend. Otherwise, and apropos of a world in strife, it would be logical for human existence to end up in chaos, or in some worse evil.

Men are in combat, or in any kind of struggle against each other, not due alone to material circumstance, but also because of different ideals. On each side of a conflict they are, in fact, willing finally to lay down their lives in what they consider to be a sufficiently good and righteous cause. Just what is the mixture that so affects the emotions?

By nature, opposites, such as good and evil, are said to be

not only contradictory, but also irreconcilable. If that be true, does it follow, or not, that the world conflict is continual, varying only in degree?

And there is another subject that we might now mention, for further example. There is discernible in man, not only a desire for absolute knowledge and a similar urge toward perfect wisdom, but also a faculty of choice. The human being can choose between different aims and courses of action, in keeping not only with ideals that are right, but also in keeping with ideals that are wrong, yet which he may, or may not, believe are right. The matter of sincerity is thus involved in our considerations.

Belief, being the complex phenomenon that it is, it is a mistake to consider all confirmed enemies, or even casual opponents, insincere, although we be convinced that they are wrong and so unworthy that, rightly, we should not trust them out of sight around a corner. And suppose they are sincere. Is sincerity, in itself, both a means and an end? Is it self-sufficient, or does sincerity require a higher, or a lower, aim than itself in order to be justified?

Or, is the question of sufficiency in such an instance merely part of a greater design of means and ends? If so, exactly what is the nature of that greater design?

Those are among the questions that we need to answer, and to answer rightly, before we have finished the present investigation.

4.

There are human characteristics that we usually take for granted and so do not always, nor often, consider carefully. As a case in point, take again the puzzling affair of the imagination.

Apparently at will, or even against his will, man can remember events of the past and can picture the times ahead. In an instant, our imaginings can span the months and years and are able to transport our thoughts with equal ease to scenes nearby or thousands of miles away. What man can imagine, he can do. What has been done, or witnessed by man, what is to be done, or otherwise experienced, can be imagined—

The skyline of Manhattan from the Staten Island ferry. The snow-mantled Jungfrau gazing majestically over Kleine Scheidegg into the future. The towering cliffs and deep ravines of the east coast of Formosa, mysterious at sundown from offshore. Banff and the sound of the Bow River Falls. Kansas wheat fields. Jet planes. Daybreak at sea in clear weather in the North Atlantic. The Honor System. Nature at rest and in motion. Safeguards against oppression.

Trafalgar Square. The bund at Shanghai. Collins Avenue and 23rd Street, Miami Beach. The assembly lines of Detroit and Los Angeles. Cotton mills in Gorizia. The industrious Scheldt at Antwerp, the spire of the Cathedral. Prestwick and Terceira, crossroads of the air. Thoughts, words and deeds, separate and interrelated. The dividing line.

George Washington in prayer at Valley Forge. The silence of the blackened and deserted battlefields of Ypres and Mount Kemmel. Light through the stained-glass windows of the Sainte Chapelle. The spirit of Texas. The blue sweep of the Smoky Mountains.

Human thought is free of the barriers of space and time— free, but in what measure?—and is restless in its search for truth.

CHAPTER TWO

Thought

THINKING is characteristic of life. All animate beings, from the one-celled amoeba, for example, to the relatively complex *homo sapiens*, seem to be able, in some measure, to think, or to engage in some such process. Plants we now only make a bow to, in passing.

Thought is discernible from its manifestations, rather than by means of direct observation of a physical mechanism. Thinking and thought are, accordingly, subjects mainly to be considered inductively. They are subjects which lend themselves to inference from particular qualities and to analogy within a general pattern.

A vague definition of thought, as some sort of implement generated by the bodily organism, as a means of adjusting itself to its environment, has been put forward from time to time. Such definition is of interest but, so far, too many mental phenomena fail to be explained thereby. In a highly respected and practical direction, laboratory research under way in various places in the world—and, in particular, at Duke University, now and during the last twenty years and more—gives a scientific basis for a belief in the existence of an "extrasensory" order of perception and of a mental force, or function of the mind, that can act directly on a physical object.

Thinking is a systematic process that ranges from instinctive acts and reactions, up scale, through degrees of the elementary and the intuitive, to deliberately conscientious and so-called elaborative thought. For any one of us, the process includes a power of decision. Thinking includes a mental ability, a free will, to choose among alternatives in the series of events that constitutes one of the records of a lifetime on earth. It involves a sequence of thoughts. And a thought, according to usually accepted definition, is an idea or mental image, a particular concept of any magnitude and importance.

It is said that man is distinguished from other animate beings, not to say lively, by the native possession of a group of faculties, each having its own special office as well as its joint function, that enables him conscientiously to tell right from wrong, and to govern himself, more or less, accordingly. Man seems to be unique in this possession, which implies imagination, the ability to imagine the ideal, to compare and identify various ideals and, also, to compare and identify the abstract, as well as the concrete, elements of a human event. It appears, from where we stand, that only man can imagine immortality, a superhuman power and a universe centered in an eternity. The mind is the stronghold of the imagination, or, in case of need, the imagination is a man's own castle.

Elementary thinking is closely related to naming, to the identification of ideas and objects by name. All words are, in fact, names. Probably no two persons ever have precisely the same view of circumstances nor give precisely the same meaning to a name. As between individuals, subjective reality is a variable. It can vary extremely or almost not at all. When a problem is under consideration it helps all around, nevertheless, if the persons concerned are reasonably sure that they are thinking of substantially the same ideas and things. Imponderables do not lend themselves well to mathematical or quantitive definition but we can still be reasonably exact if, at the same time, relatively arbitrary, at first.

These pages take the arbitrary position, for example, that each mental faculty can be divided into two contrasting states, or phases, namely, a state of equilibrium as of a given moment, and, second, a corresponding mental process that involves change. In other words, it is assumed that each mental faculty is capable of both an active, or kinetic, and a potential, or passive, phase. Memory is one of the mental faculties. The state of equilibrium, or the condition of memory, may vary from moment to moment. Memorizing and remembering are processes of memory. That statement is, however, let us note, an oversimplification, since all the faculties, of which the total number may be still unknown, can be assumed to work together in any ordinary form of thought.

A definition of the "mind" is necessary for present purposes. As a first idea on the subject, the mind seems to be an integration of intangible and tangible elements. The mind is the familiar instrument of human thought, in that, unseen, like thought itself, it makes its presence known by its systematic workings. At the same time, it operates in conjunction with the brain. The mechanism of the mind appears to be located precisely enough in and around the brain, but it seems also to function in a likewise invisible field that is limitless in time and space, yet bound by natural law. Everything that man feels, discerns, knows and believes, all thinking, is by means of the mind.

And, now that we are here, there can be set forth without more ado, a few other definitions, among the many that are needed.

Knowledge is the aggregate of facts and figures, truth and skill, acquired or retained by the mind in any process and from any source, the sum total of native intelligence and all that has been learned. Wisdom is "the right use of knowledge," an important distinction indeed between the two.

The human will, closely allied to other faculties, such as reason and choice, leads to the power of self-control and of perseverance. It is the ability, actual or potential, of controlling one's own actions, one's personal feelings and thoughts, especially by deliberate choice, as compared to decision by default. The projection of the will of one person into the affairs of another is also a phenomenon of life.

And the brain—happily for the skeptic and the agnostic, photographs can be taken of it—the brain, as the physical organ of the mind, is the control tower of the muscular and nervous systems of the body and of other bodily mechanisms that are contrived to maintain a balance of their own, contrived not only to interact among themselves, but also to work with other and different elements of mental organization and activity.

I am assured, meanwhile, by expert opinion, that no one knows what kind of natural phenomenon thought is, that, scientifically, there is not even a theory in that regard.

This leaves us quite an open field, to put it mildly. Rather than wander over the lot in all directions at once, it would be well, in this chapter on "thought," to list some aspects of the subject with which we should deal, particularly in the next few pages.

It is proposed, then, first to look back briefly on human experience, by way of getting our relative position lined up, to date, and of glancing also at a few ideas and analogies along the route. Second, the need is clear to have a further look at the mind itself, its component parts and how the parts seem likely to work, and to work best, together. Objective and subjective reality are sure to come up now and again, as is also the matter of the contrasting planes of thought that are discernible. And, third, the forms in which thought manifests itself to us should bring the search to the question of the nature of thought itself, to the phenomenon of the mind's conscious and unconscious cycle and to the subject of the interrelation of the potential and active phases of thought.

In connection with the various capabilities and impacts of thought, including the power of suggestion, which is akin to the force of example, and also including such concepts as private property, preparedness, law and order, and other matters that also involve the different realities in a system of reward and punishment, you can imagine, of course, how the . . . but that might be looking too far ahead, for the moment.

2.

About the past, we are told by generally accepted authorities on such subjects, of the evidence that our planet, the Earth, has been in existence for nobody knows how long and that it has been habitable by animate beings, beginning with elementary forms of vegetable and animal life, for a billion five-hundred million, or as much as two billion years or more.

Primitive man is said to have made his appearance on the worldly scene some hundreds of thousands, or up to a million years ago—probably to have emerged from the run-of-the-mill of animate beings, between 250,000 and 400,000 years before now. The million years in question represents the most recent geological period, the Pleistocene, in which we still live today. The Pleistocene period, or epoch, is the most recent million years of the Cenozoic era, the era in which the mammals came into their own.

For the record, the approximately two billion years of the

Earth's more or less habitable existence is divided, geologically, as follows—with the estimated durations and paleontological ages indicated, respectively:

a. The Archeozoic and Proterozoic eras, the first and second grand divisions of geological time; duration, 1,500,000,-000 years.

In, say, the first 500 million years of the total duration of these eras, the Earth was probably still in molten form and rocks had not yet been deposited. It was a period followed by the Archean and Algonkian Ages, now evidencing only traces of living organisms, both plant and invertebrate animal.

b. The Paleozoic era, the first period of which is known as the Cambrian; duration 335,000,000 years. In this era there were the Ages of Fishes and Amphibians, respectively.

c. The Mesozoic era; duration 125,000,000 years; the Age of Reptiles.

d. The Cenozoic era; duration, 60,000,000 years, so far. This is the present era, which we had already mentioned. It is the Age of Mammals.

There are, also, the archaeological divisions of time, which, beginning with man's earliest appearance, comprise, in turn, the Stone Age, the Copper, Bronze and Iron Ages and so on, up to the present age of whatever it ends up by being called. The Stone Age is divided into two periods, namely, the Old Stone Age, or the Paleolithic, and the New Stone Age, or Neolithic. The earliest part of the Paleolithic Age is also known as the Eolithic.

Returning to the present age, geologically, there has also been another classification of age that has characterized the Pleistocene epoch, namely, the Ice Age. It might be better to say the Ice Ages. There have been great glacial and interglacial periods, advances and retreats of great ice caps, lasting altogether as much as 250,000 years or more. The last glacial period, or Ice Age, ended, it is believed, some 15,000 years ago. Perhaps we are in an interglacial period today. At times during these Ages, ice is said to have covered as much as one-sixth of the surface of the Earth.

In North America, for instance, the ice sheets covered, at one time and another, all of what is now Canada and a large part of the northern areas of the United States. The ice extended southward to a line runing west from New Jersey to the banks of the Ohio and Missouri Rivers, approximately, and then through Montana and Idaho, to the Pacific Coast. Several kinds of elephant, including the mammoth and the mastodon, have roamed the North American scene during the Pleistocene epoch. And, elephants aside, if you had travelled around these parts from time to time, before and during some of the Ice Ages, you would have been just as likely to run into a giant armadillo, or a sabre-tooth cat, or a camel, or a ground sloth, as you would have been to meet a bison, or a wolf, or a wild pig.

As long ago as 25,000 and 50,000 years, man left numerous traces of his existence in a savage state, that is, in a stage of development in which he preyed on nature for a day-to-day subsistence. He left such reminders on every continent and in many islands of the Earth. Old Stone Age relics include such things as simple paintings and drawings, pottery, flints for arrowheads, rough stone tools, and primitive weapons, and also that versatile instrument, the axe, not to mention articles of personal adornment and comparatively well-assorted bones. And the traces indicate that, early in the Old Stone Age, man had learned to control, or partly to control, fire.

From the shores of the Mediterranean Sea and the Indian Ocean to Great Britain, from Switzerland and France and Germany to the Ukraine, from South Africa to Afghanistan, from Siberia and China to Australia and the Americas—to use modern names—primitive man had begun to leave signs of the modest beginnings of his upward climb. In North America, for example, recent archaeological excavations in Nebraska, the Dakotas and elsewhere in the Missouri River basin, have uncovered sites of camps and villages. These prehistoric dwelling places are classified, according to type of relics, as those of Early Hunters, probably predating the transitional phase, archaeologically, that followed close upon the latest Ice Age.

The relatively brief New Stone Age is distinguished from the lengthy Old Stone Age by the sharpened stone tools that were made by grinding or polishing the edges, as compared with the blunt and chipped, or flaked, stones used in the Old Stone Age. It took man hundreds of thousands of years to learn *deliberately* to sharpen the edges of stone implements for a chosen purpose. It took him millennia to grasp consciously the principle involved in the deliberate act. His implements then began to permit carpentering, plowing and other new activities. The way was opened, and soon led, to urban development and to a knowledge of the metals and of other arts and crafts.

The progress of human communities in the New Stone Age is also now evidenced, materially, in the form of conventional signs and meanings, interpretable records, including, at the dawn of history, picture writing, such as the sacred drawings, or hieroglyphics, of the Ancient Egyptians and the cuniform inscriptions of the Sumerians and the Babylonians.

A later development has included ideograms of the kind that are still used in writing Chinese languages. And, in addition to records of that order and to the actual remains of some of the contemporary Neolithic humans themselves, there are other relics of the period that extended into the Copper Age, relics such as contrivances based on the simple mechanical principles of the wedge and of the lever. In the Middle East of 5,000 to 10,000 B.C., the wheeled cart, the sailboat, the hoe and the plow had been invented, or discovered. There are, likewise, relics of religious rites, as there are also of such rites in the Old Stone Age.

The Neolithic transition seems to have begun comparatively soon after the latest Ice Age, or, say, somewhat over 10,000 years before now. In one form of recording or another —geological, archaeological, biological, or historical, or whatever the approach may be—human life, by the time of such transition, already indicated the existence of a social pattern. The general pattern of wishes, of drives and urges toward supremacy and toward final perfection, and away from indecision and chaos, has persisted and has evolved, from the savagery and the barbarism of the Stone Age economies, through the Copper, Bronze and Iron Ages, respectively, to the highly complex civilizations which we are so apt to take for granted in our day.

Within the general framework of human development, varied evidences of the growth of various cultures have been found in divers places. As was to have been expected in view of the importance of the variety of circumstance in the scheme of life, there have been changing social, political and other orders. There have been growths at different rates of advancement in different parts of the world.

When, in the 16th century A.D., the Spanish *conquistadores* arrived in the New World, now known as the Americas, they found that even the more advanced of the native peoples, such as the Aztecs and the Incas—the more civilized, if you like—for all of their imposing edifices and ceremonial customs, were barely in a stage of transition from the economies of the Stone Age to the economies of the Copper and Bronze Ages. The natives rarely used beasts of burden. Surprising as it may now seem, the wheel and axle—and, like-wise, writing—were unknown to them until the arrival of the Europeans. At the beginning of the present century, as another illustration, some tribes of Central Africa were still in a paleolithic stage of development.

I do not know what good this kind of general information does us, except as a matter of perspective and of knowing as much as we can from which to draw general conclusions or by which to support theories. Man instinctively has curiosity, especially about anything affecting himself, an urge to know why and how to go ahead in one direction or the other. The information may be useful in pointing to the fact, for instance, that it is the principle of human development, or the force of an ideal, that is of paramount importance, rather than unrecognizable place and climate, no matter how exciting the thought of such circumstances may be, and rather than the measurement of time in terms of days, or centuries, or millennia.

Specifically, as perspective, after trying to think in billions, it brings the Sphinx into a friendly yesterday to know that it is now only about 5000 years old. And, until I studied up on such things, I always wondered where all those "barbarians" came from who were continually beating against the northern boundaries of Rome. I still wonder, but not quite so vaguely as heretofore.

Notable, insofar as the main current of western civilization has been and is concerned, there is the ancient development of the human community in the river valleys of the Middle East, namely, in the valley of the Tigris and the Euphrates, and in the valley of the Nile. I suppose that the same could be said, but in a lesser degree, of the valley of the Indus.

For example, the Sumerians were a people who emerged a few thousand years ago, from savagery into barbarism, in the area of Mesopotamia at the mouth of the Euphrates. In this general region, excavations have been made during the present century at the site of the ancient city of Ur. The findings there, as also elsewhere, have helped to piece together the story of the past. If barbarism be taken to mean an intermediate stage of development in the direction of civilization, a state characterized by a primitive coöperation with nature as compared with the depredations of savagery, then the people of Sumer, like any people, emerged from savagery into barbarism when they began to make use of the laws of nature by an obedience and loyalty thereto on a systematic scale. They built villages that grew into such organized communities as cities.

All of Sumeria was brought together politically, with Semitic elements added from adjacent regions, in a further development of the workings of sovereignty, under the rule of Sargon, King of Akkad, about 2800 B.C. His kingdom was the forerunner of Babylonian power. His conquests disclosed a pattern of empire that was to become familiar as time went on. The Sumerians are chosen for particular mention here because of their custom of meeting in council, as a people, to deliberate concerning affairs of common interest.

I have before me, as I write, a printed translation of words taken from a record that dates back to the Egypt of about 2600 B.C.—the earliest extant writings, it is said, of an Egypt then many dynasties old. The pyramids of Egypt were begun about 3000 years B.C. By then, copper was beginning to be smelted and a solar calendar had been worked out. There are, likewise, available inscriptions and fragments of the written thoughts of the Babylon of two millennia before the beginning of the Christian era. Human history, in the generally accepted meaning of the words, began around 5000 years ago.

Memorable dates of ancient times have to be set with considerable leeway. Authorities differ as much as two or three hundred years, or more, in regard to dates of the earliest recorded history, including dates such as those already mentioned in the preceding paragraph above. For example, from data now available, the estimates of when Moses lived vary from, say, 1200 to 1450 years before Christ. The psalms of David, King of Israel, were first sung about a thousand years B.C.

All dates in this paragraph being B.C., Homer flourished, so it seems, around 850, or earlier. The legendary date of the founding of Rome by Romulus is 753. Gautama Buddha, in India, and Confucius, in China, were contemporaries of the 6th century. Aesop and his fables are of the vintage of 550, followed in a few decades by Democritus and his mental image of the atom. Plato was born about 427, some forty years later than Socrates and some forty years before his famous pupil, Aristotle. Alexander the Great, of Macedon, had conquered his world by 323. Aristotle, for a time, had been Alexander's tutor. The Rome of the Republic became the Roman Empire, under Augustus Caesar, less than a half-century before the birth of Christ.

And, *annibus domini*, we have room now for only three or four of the many great names that could be remembered to advantage because of good works. In addition to Saint Paul, who lived until about A.D. 67, we can mention Saint Augustine who was born in 354. Justinian, Emperor of the East, codified the Roman law at the middle of the 6th century. The Hegira of Mahomet, the Prophet of Islam, took place in 622. It would be easier to keep on listing one more name, and then another, of great or lesser stature among those who have influenced profoundly the thought and deed of their fellow men. Some of them should be referred to elsewhere in the course of the discussion.

Mankind has, today, the heritage of contrasting and enduring philosophies of century-old civilizations, the abstract thought, the beauty and civic pride of Ancient Greece, the example of the early Roman citizen's devotion to strength and usefulness, his sense of duty as the steward of power and possessions entrusted to him by his household gods and by his country's deities.

We take for granted the English alphabet and Arabic numerals, as if they were not great inventions or great discoveries. We have the infinite advantage of the highest religious concepts and of the almost incredible progress of the last few hundred years in the scientific field. Man has mastered the fission of the atom, with all that the now well-proven theory of relativity implies philosophically as well as scientifically—implies, for instance, against the attainability of perfection, physically, in the realm of space and time.

But, at mid-20th century, it seems that no one knows what kind of natural phenomenon thought is! No wonder a human community such as our own, makes big mistakes now and then in trying to govern itself when we do not know what we are thinking with.

And what, by the way, is our definition of "nature"? In the recent age of materialism a habit was developed of disassociating the immaterial and the natural. But maybe thought is not a physical phenomenon alone, not a natural phenomenon in the sense that nature is only physical. Without getting mixed up in pantheism, maybe thought is as all-pervading as nature itself, as nature philosophically defined and scientifically considered to be "the totality of powers, or agencies, which determine the character and the process of things in general and in detail."

3.

This book is concerned with thought and with the nature and the laws of existence and reality, with science and philosophy and with religious principle, from the standpoint of human sovereignty, including not only the source of sovereign power but also the actual governmental system and the courses of action, the ways and means, that lead to lasting political supremacy. The scope of the present inquiry is intended to be limited, as well as extended, accordingly.

The present author makes no claim to be a scientist, a theologian or a professional philosopher. In fact, he must admit that he often has considerable difficulty in remembering what which philosopher has said, or even which the philosopher is who has said what.

But, at least, he leans toward Shakespeare, Robert Burns and Tennyson, toward G. A. Henty's sense of the historical and Walt Disney's artistry—and toward the Proverbs of Solomon—rather than in the direction of the elaborate and, often as not, self-contradictory theories of Kant and John Stuart Mill. Objective and subjective reality must be in agreement with each other, and simply so, if there is to be peace of mind. For such well-balanced thought, in the form, for instance, of a mixture of solid fact and sound fantasy, he has been inclined to follow Joel Chandler Harris and, more recently, the ideas and illustrations of Harold Gray and of V. T. Hamlin. He automatically mistrusts some of the ideas expressed by the late John Dewey.

Beyond rambling comment, however, the economic, social and political theory of Karl Marx (1818-1883) is another thing again. In his theory of interpreting human existence in terms of economic cause and effect in an atheistic world where the supreme power is physical, Marx hit upon a concept of materialism that presents the exact opposite of a worshipful belief in God. The rise of communism and the powerful soviet socialist state is indication enough that the theory developed by Marx, his associate, Friedrich Engels, and their successors—including unsuspecting allies, such as the late Lord Keynes, to mention only one—should be examined carefully, the better to be opposed and offset. Karl Marx is mentioned now, so that we can begin thinking about his ideas again, in view of the mention which various aspects of his theory will require in the present volume.

Sometimes the ruminations of scientists can be even more intriguing to consider than those of philosophers, not that there is always an entirely clear boundary between these two realms of thought. If intricate formulas and formidable equations be taken to stand at face value, there is much of general, as well as special, interest in reading about the advance of knowledge concerning mathematics, for example, particularly in the way of analogy thereto in the fields even of political economy and the social order.

In science, take, for example, Planck's theory of energy quanta, or units—Max Karl Ernest Ludwig Planck, the German physicist—the theory that has led, in our day, to quantum theories of matter, electricity and light, as well as of energy. All truths of physical science carry interesting, if, at the same time, limited, analogies in respect to natural laws governing probabilities, and changes in probabilities, as pertinent to human behavior in the aggregate, or, say, as pertinent to the predictable behavior of a majority of people and the unpredictability of some individuals, in a large commonwealth, or social mass. There are such analogies, at least, from the standpoint of the mathematics of chance, of chance as uninfluenced by human choice in the light of a guiding principle of human thought.

And, one more theory I would call to your attention, before ending this part of the present excursion. It remains to mention the astronomer, Copernicus, and his theory of the solar system.

Suffice it, for present purposes, to set forth briefly that Nicholas Copernicus (1473-1543) was born in a Polish province, then part of Prussia. He was born into a world that, since the 2nd century A.D., had generally accepted the Ptolemaic system of astronomy based on a theory evolved by Ptolemy, a celebrated Graeco-Egyptian mathematician, geographer and astronomer of Alexandria, that the sun, planets and stars revolve around the Earth. Parenthetically, this was a thought, we now know, in which subjective reality did not agree entirely with the truth. It was an accepted idea that lasted, nevertheless, for more than a thousand years.

There was much dissatisfaction with the Ptolemaic system, especially when seafarers ventured into the great oceans beyond the gate of the Mediterranean Sea. A story is told of King Alphonso X, of Castile, who reigned in the 13th century A.D., and who went to great ends to overcome the difficulties inherent in the Ptolemaic theory. His efforts in that direction were by means of complicated, mathematical figurings and adjustments that were compiled in 1252, and are known as the Alphonsine Tables. The force of habit, the lack of imagination, or vested interest, or something, held back for centuries the discovery of the true astronomical theory. King Alphonso, however, went so far as to say, "Had I been at the creation I would have given some useful hints for the better ordering of the Universe." A number of persons seem to feel the same way about the universe today.

And, in the 20th century A.D., there is not even a theory about what kind of a natural phenomenon a cycle of thought is.

The story about Copernicus comes to a happy ending, as we know, except that he passed from the mortal scene, like so many other people, without having accomplished all that he had wanted and hoped to do. His theory of the solar system coincided with objective reality, as of the immediate scale of observation, and came so near the truth that, ever afterward, men have had peace of mind, at least on one subject—the Earth turns daily on its axis and the planets revolve in their orbits around the sun.

4.

You get out of life what you put in it, the saying goes. Be that as it will, you get out of your mind what your mind has in itself.

And your mind has in it its native endowment, together with what you have accepted to go in it, accepted as important or unimportant, as theory or fact, as true or false, accepted for some cause, good or bad, because of some choice, right or wrong.

To have the further look at the mind and at the nature of thought, which we promised ourselves some pages ago, there are discernible two elementary planes of thought. They are usually termed, respectively, the physical and the spiritual.

Plane, in this sense, seems to be a convenient, though motionless, term. But there are, say, two mutually contrasting planes, or areas, or fields, or realms of nature, each with its own quality, concepts and activities, areas which represent separate and, at the same time, inseparably related parts of the same thing, namely, of thought.

These planes of thought, call them what we will, can be identified respectively, and compared with each other in terms of opposites, under various names. For example, there are such opposites as the tangible and the intangible, the visible and the invisible, the concrete and the abstract, the temporal and the eternal, the material and the immaterial—but there is another distinction that is more personal.

The physical is primarily the field of the body, of the mental processes that have to do with the material plane. The spiritual seems to relate, first of all, to the soul, to the spark of eternal existence that is an element of each human being.

In addition, there is recognizable an intermediate field, or area, which is known as the moral plane. It partakes of the various attributes of the two elementary planes. Intuition, as well as actual observation, tells us that the spiritual ideal and the physical circumstance are brought together systematically in the issues of the moral plane of everyday affairs.

As a preliminary to thinking further, in due course, about the differences among the planes of thought, our first definition of the mind can now be extended.

It is in the mind that the body and soul are joined. The soul and body are indivisibly joined in thought, in the mind. It is only in terms jointly of the body and the soul that the day-to-day phenomena of each can be explained fully in the mind by thought.

The mind is the common meeting-place of concepts, or ideas, from the mutually contrasting planes of thought; it is the workshop in which the physical and spiritual elements of man's thinking are brought together to form concepts of human morality. The mind, the heart and the soul, indivisible, constitute the human being, the individual human.

To go a step further, the mind is the instrument of thought, in respect to knowledge and wisdom, both conscious and unconscious. Functioning in a system of opposites, each mental faculty and, similarly, the mind as a whole, seems to have its unconscious as well as its conscious phases.

No complete distinction is to be made with certainty, at present, if ever, among the different forms, or degrees, or phases of consciousness, such as those termed, for example, the preconscious and the subconscious. This book but wishes that it could explain the possibly obvious enough part played by sleep in the system of human thinking. It does not propose to draw a dividing line between the conscious and the unconscious mind.

For reference, nevertheless, we can make an assumption, if we want to, that the unconscious is the field of ideals and ideas that have been accepted by a mind, as true, including originally the natural concepts of perfection that are common to each member of the race. In addition, we can assume that, in the course of living, the unconscious is also the field where further ideas considered by the conscious mind of anyone to be probably worthy of acceptance into his mind, as truth and fact, may have finally to struggle for the upper hand over the opposition of concepts which already hold current or permanent sway therein. Ideals struggle continually for supremacy in the human mind. It is in the unconscious mind, it seems, that final decisions are made.

If, by the way, we were to accept a premise that truth is naturally sovereign in the unconscious or, in other words, that truth is, by nature, sovereign, then the idealizing of a falsehood constitutes a serious, even a paralyzing, conflict, rather than a reversal of opinion in the unconscious. For, apropos of peace of mind, the truth remains always unchanged.

The paramount conflict in human life is for men's minds and thoughts. The conflict is personal. The course of history can be changed by the outcome of a battle for a ruler's mind. And the ruler may be either an individual, or a minority group, or the will of the majority of the citizens in a community, such as the United States.

It would be easier than it would be warranted, to assume abruptly that thought and nature and existence are exactly the same phenomenon, although they may well turn out to be manifestations of the same thing, all three arising from the same source. It is not too much, however, now to note that human thoughts, like human lives and human nature, always play the dual role of contrast.

By way of an analogy to scientific concepts, such as those supporting the quantum theory of energy, for instance—a theory that is readily accepted today as reasonable and, in fact, as true—thought, as a sequence of ideas, manifests itself in a system of opposites, not only recurrently but also discontinuously, in units, or, say, in individual packages, as may be said similarly of events.

As compared with nothingness, or the opposite of existence, every energy in being is essentially good. Goodness and good will are terms for the nature of existence. Every thought that corresponds to natural law is essentially good. It is in this sense that the force of existence makes use of the energy of thought and is the moving spirit of human nature.

To man, the laws of thought resemble the laws of nature and of existence itself. In keeping with the concept of Relativity, the idea and the energy can be viewed as different, but mutually sustaining, forms of the same thing, namely, the force of thought—the force through which, by the instrument of the mind, existence makes itself known to the human being.

5.

It is a temptation at this point to exercise the inalienable right of taking off into the wild blue yonder of an unsupported flight or two of the imagination.

It is a temptation, but no—not without an eye to the consequences. According to the preface of this book, if we go up, our flights should not be such as to invite crash landings. Man can imagine nearly anything, but, actually, his successful flights are within the reliable bounds of nature's laws.

A little while ago, we left in mid-air an idea that thought might not be merely a phenomenon of physical nature. We should not neglect to view this idea in clearer perspective on a more substantial basis. A good place to do so could be under the heading of our next chapter. We might then advance a different theory, even a theory of our own, in regard to the nature of thought.

In any event, "thought" is a subject which is bound to be in mind throughout the whole course of the present argument. This early discussion is mostly by way of recalling a few facts. And there are now also some clues to further facts about thought, some indications to be examined briefly and, at least, noted for the record.

In the physical realm, for example, what is potential energy, as of a given place and moment, or, say, as of here and now? Potential energy seems to occupy no point of space nor instant of time, but the fact of the existence of potential energy is accepted in our thoughts, and its physical power can be estimated systematically. The electron, the elementary particle, or quantum, of matter has no mass. The same is true of the photon, the elementary unit of energy.

Occupying no space nor time, potential energy puts itself into the category of an abstraction.

Is potential energy, physically, of the same nature as the force of an ideal, that is waiting to be brought down to earth by the outriders of the imagination and put to work in day-to-day affairs on the moral plane? As an indication of a reasonable answer, it is axiomatic that, wherever work is done, an energy is present.

Does the respective thinking in the conscious and the unconscious realms of the mind represent the kinetic and potential phases of an unseen, but mighty, power? We observe that nature moves in cycles. We discern that human thinking, as also human life, revolves in phases with a trend, or line of progress in one direction or the other.

Now it is not intended to imply a complete analogy between the phenomena of thought and the mathematical workings of, for example, the physical solar system. A complete analogy of that kind would not allow for such imponderables as human decision. Mechanistically, it could lead to all sorts of ideas, such as transmigration of the soul and reincarnation—or to the concept of an absorption into the infinite, whatever that vague process might be.

But the physical example is intended to draw attention to an analogy in the matter of a dynamic system of existence centered on a source of strength.

6.

So it is true that, for mankind, thought is the common denominator of all phenomena—and man can afford to sit around all day, thinking good thoughts to himself, and do little else than filling himself full of potential good will?

Maybe. That may be just the thing to do, and probably is just the thing to do, at least part of the time. There are many ways and means of making progress toward perfection.

Perfection of thought may well have to come before perfection of the deed. It would appear right, nevertheless, that a thought, in order to fulfill its being, needs an active, as well as a passive, phase, that good thoughts alone are not always, if ever, enough for human progress in the right direction.

For in truly good thought it should be clear, on its own evidence, that rightly chosen ideas should be put to work in daily affairs by deeds of essentially the same good character as that of the ideas themselves.

Since thought, in terms of ideas, is discontinuous, as well as recurrent, good intentions alone are not enough. The character of the intent, as of here and now, does not necessarily determine the character of the consequences of a thought, or word, or deed, of even the best intention. Integrity needs to be preserved, idea by idea, step by step.

Perfection seems to be always beyond, not only the reach of the wrong decision, but also beyond the mathematics of haphazard choice or, in other words, of chance. It can be reasoned, from strong premises, that the idea and the deed must sustain and strengthen each other continually, not just now and then, if steady and enduring progress is to be made toward the correspondingly well-balanced aim.

In the moral realm of thought there is raised, then, an ideal according to which we should always know good ways how, as well as good reasons why, and why as well as how. And that really cuts out a nice piece of work for anyone who is interested, for instance, in principle and power, in politics, supremacy and peace.

Part II

Principle and Power

CHAPTER THREE

The General Theory of
Benevolent Supremacy

POLITICS is the science and art of government. It is the science that deals with the organization, regulation and administration of a state, or similar body, in both its external and its internal affairs. Take, for example, our own nation with its domestic and foreign affairs, the two areas of national policy that are essentially inseparable, that are always interrelated in some degree as are also the individual and community interests of human society.

Supremacy has to do with superiority in respect to quality, or quantity, or both. To be supreme is actually to be predominant to the highest degree. Supremacy implies a mastery of the situation in such manner as to hold the upper hand of all comers in the field. As among human beings or communities, there is no such thing as an absolute supremacy. It is, rather, a matter of effective ascendancy, an ascendance that is practically a supremacy.

A political authority, effectively established as supreme within the area of its authority, is a sovereign power. It is axiomatic that, in order to remain sovereign, a political authority, such as the authority of a nation, must be able to maintain law and order within the area of its established rule.

A human sovereignty, in order continually to pursue successfully a chosen course in a desired direction, must keep the upper hand of the threats to its existence, either from within or from outside its own boundaries.

The current of events in human life on the Earth includes phenomena of movement and of trend among opposing forces. It is a life of changing circumstance in a system of reward and punishment governed by changeless law. It is within such framework that the immediate problem facing us is to choose an initial hypothesis. We need a starting point from which to develop a theory of the nature of the force which is supreme.

Historically, there are two main methods for us to choose between in developing a theory, namely, the deductive and the inductive methods. The two methods differ in their respective ways of putting facts to use. They differ also in their respective approaches to a theoretical conclusion.

To look first at the deductive method, it assumes that a theory is to be drawn from the facts. It assumes that the facts, comprising objects of direct experience and other truths directly related to events, are there to speak for themselves, without benefit of preconceived conclusions. It reasons primarily from the particular to the general, from particular facts to the general finding.

Deductive reasoning can go beyond a superficial look at facts, and is immensely important in man's thinking. But, for instance, in regard to the human being, the human community and the human event, caution is more than advisable in generalizing.

There are imponderables resulting from environment, from education and varied experience. Different persons, different communities, different nationals, have different points of view. The fact is there, in any case—the same fact, no matter how it be related or employed—but there is bound to be a formidable margin of error in the lengthy process of trying only to deduce a reliable theory from innumerable facts.

Generally speaking, theory, as compared with hypothesis, is taken to be a formula which has undergone verification, and which has been found to be applicable to a large number of related phenomena.

Theory and theater, by the way, are words which have a common ancestor in the Greek noun *thea*, sight, or in its verb form, to see, to view. *Theoria* is a beholding, or a speculation. Good theater, we say, rings true. We could say the same of good theory.

The second of the two methods above referred to, namely, the inductive, keeps in mind the formal difference between theory and hypothesis. At the same time, it chooses an initial proposition which gives evidence of being, not only an imaginative and reasonable hypothesis, but also a true theory.

This method then proceeds to make use of facts and, insofar as possible, of the findings of actual experiment to test the hypothesis, or preconceived conclusion, as to its being a valid theory. In contrast to the deductive, the inductive method makes a definite assumption of the truth in advance of detailed proof.

The initial hypothesis may turn out to be true, or false. Even if it be true, it can represent, like Galileo's theory of the solar system, only a firm step forward in the right direction, only an element of, instead of the whole, truth. But in any event, during the process of testing the proposition, including the study of what follows from the proposition, the initial hypothesis itself needs to remain unchallenged.

This is in order to discover an integrated system on the assumption that what really follows from the true hypothesis is true, and that what conflicts with the true hypothesis is false. Polaris needs to remain the pole-star throughout the entire proceedings. The relative alone is not enough.

It is proposed to use primarily the second of the indicated methods, the inductive method, during the present inquiry into supremacy and into the workings of sovereign power, or to try to follow such method. If any of us weaken, or are thrown off going around a curve during the present proceedings, we can console ourselves. We can encourage ourselves to try again by remembering that, in clinging to our chosen method and in pursuing thereby the development of a theory, we have been in good company.

We are in such excellent company as Socrates and Sir Isaac Newton and, among discoverers in more recent years, Lord Rutherford, who, following Becquerel's findings in the field of radioactivity and atomic structure, was the first man to split the atom — and may the results of our clinging be to approach such a standard!

2.

If, as assumed in one of our notes on an earlier page, "good" be taken to be any idea that strengthens the urge toward perfect existence, then another name for a force of this nature is "good will." In our world, the good idea and its corresponding will, or force, can be said to work together in a common purpose of achieving all-around goodness, or perfection. If the elements of life in our world are representative of the universe, then, aside from any play on words, good will turns out to be essentially the force of existence itself.

In the abstract, the force of existence, in order for existence to endure in the future as in the past and present, needs eternally to have an effective supremacy over opposition to its will. Existence, or good, is, by nature, a supremacy of its own force, or will. Concretely, if still in general terms, human existence is, by nature, a supremacy of good will. By way of preliminary, this is a statement characterizing the general theory of benevolent supremacy, a theory applicable to a benevolent sovereignty in any field.

We are out to test the truth of the general theory, along with various special theories which we are likely to formulate from time to time, while considering the actual implementation of the general concept.

For instance, there is the matter of a special theory of political sovereignty. In the universe there is discernible a force which, if put to use energetically and systematically in accordance with its natural design, tends to strengthen within the human community the influence of the ideals from which the force springs.

Meanwhile, the phenomena can be noted, here and now, that good will is essentially the force of an idea and, also in accordance with our previous observations, that ideas take form for the human being through, and by the use of, his various mental faculties in the process of thinking.

Without ideas, a universe, or even an earthly existence in the world which we can observe, would be unimaginable indeed and apparently unnatural. The reason that existence is the only concept which has no opposite is that it is impossible to imagine nothingness. Or, so it can be said for more than argument, insofar as humans are concerned.

We are back again to the question of the respective relationships among thought and nature and existence. The eventual record of our inquiry about good government, for instance, seems likely to be anything but integrated, unless we can get a clear and constantly reliable idea of the true nature of thought. It appears to be in this area of the presumably unknown, that we need especially to choose our initial hypothesis which is to remain unchallenged, at least by us, while we are considering what follows from the proposition itself.

To go out on a limb, then, a well-worn limb which is also a vantage point, and, among other faculties, to use memory and the imagination while we are there, thought is not just an implement generated by the body as a means of the body's adjusting itself to its environment. "Thought," as compared with the actual process which we call "thinking," is one great concept originating, not within, but beyond human being, a concept common to the existence of every spark of life in the universe. And innumerable parts of the great concept as a whole can be discerned in the more or less truthful imagery of the human mind.

Thought is the form in which existence manifests itself, and manifests the nature of its laws, to animate beings. Existence is the source of thought. In its ideal state, a perfect state of knowledge and wisdom, thought is the finite integration of an infinity of concepts in regard to existing perfectly forever. And, in keeping with this point of view, there is an important distinction to be made between thought and the mind.

The mind is the instrument of the animate being by which it thinks, by which the being is continually related and characteristically attuned to thought. The actual instrument, and apparently its potential also, differs for each variety of animate existence. The instrument also differs in efficiency as between individuals of each variety, and there are contrasts in environment and in care.

Among the minds of animate beings, the human mind appears to be capable of the greatest degree of understanding in regard to thought, in whole and in part. In addition to sensing its physical circumstances, the human mind can conceive of eternity and of one principle common to all being. But the fact remains, that the mind, not thought itself, is the instrument of the human being, for adjusting the development of his life to the laws of nature which apply to him as the laws of his existence.

And that reminds me to go on record that, if the present volume in its observations often uses the masculine pronoun alone, such use is only in the interests of brevity rather than of exactness. This book does not intend to let the feminine contingent of mankind get away, especially on a technicality.

Rays of light strike the optic nerve and cause a mental perception which is known as sight. The mind evaluates scenes and puts them to use, but the eye physically does not originate nor project sight. Thoughts come into the mind. The apparatus of the mind does not originate thought but, through thinking, it can put ideas to good use, or the contrary.

Thought's forces and energies, spiritual and physical, play upon the instrument of the mind, including the mental faculty of choice. It seems more than likely that Descartes—René Descartes (1596-1650), French philosopher and scientist—with his famous words, *cogito, ergo sum,* "I think, therefore I am," has been misleading, as well as wrong in a number of ways, all these years. The line should be turned around to read: I am, therefore I think, *sum, ergo cogito.*

In a continual and ever-changing array of circumstances, ideas containing the truth are waiting to be discovered and explored, to be revealed and to be communicated from one being to another. The truth is there in any case. Human thinking can not change the truth. Mechanical devices and integrated policies of government, no less than unknown places, are waiting to be discovered, not created, by man.

To think is for the mind to explore thought. To think is

to explore and to discover, to identify, to compare, and to choose between the contrasts and the opposites which are to be found in the various fields of thought. The purpose of thinking is to add to the mind's store of knowledge and of wisdom, but not just as an exercise for the sake of exercise. Such purpose is in order to make the best use possible of revelation and of personal discovery as a means of progressing toward the ideal of perfect existence, which is inherent in the great concept of thought itself.

When we come to compare further the elements of subjective and objective reality, which, in passing, we mentioned some time ago, we still have to think more about the fact of false imaginings and of mixtures of truth and falsehood. Sooner or later, we shall also need to identify first-hand, as our forebears ever since paleolithic times have needed to do, the master design, or prototype, of the system in which the forces and energies discerned by the mind can be put to use successfully.

In our next chapter, let us aim to see how the scheme and pattern of existence begins to shape up in our present thinking, not only as a test of our initial hypothesis regarding the subject of benevolent supremacy, but also as a design common in one form or another to every kind of system that is inclined to work well.

Beforehand, we can now add in substance to the preliminary terms of our general theory above set forth.

Human existence is, by nature, a supremacy of good will. In human life, good will is the force of one great concept of perfection which manifests itself in many ways, a concept originating, not within, but beyond human being. This is the force which must be predominant in the earthly affairs of the human community, not only as a prerequisite of man's being and of his progress toward perfection, but also as a final requisite of the continued existence of the human species hereabouts.

Or, to bring the proposition into political perspective, we can state the general theory of benevolent supremacy, as follows:

Benevolent supremacy is more than a good idea, it is also a moral supremacy—and a moral supremacy depends for its existence on the use of both spiritual force and physical energy. In order for there to be a benevolent supremacy within a community, it is necessary for the sovereign power therein to have the upper hand spiritually as well as physically *and* physically as well as spiritually.

CHAPTER FOUR

The Scheme and Pattern of Reality

THERE is one fact of life on the Earth about which there is general agreement. Living is not always, if ever, an easy business. Why?

If this book had to answer that persistent question it would say that the best place to begin to look for a satisfactory explanation of the fact at point is likely to be in the scheme of reality as a whole. It is in the design of existence in its entirety that a good explanation is to be found. The answer is not a detached item of interest, nor a piece of information.

Any idea or any act, any plan or event or condition, must be considered in due context in order for its full implications to be realized and weighed. Some events are more fortunate than they seem, at first, to be. There is no use in denying that some situations, in themselves alone, are beyond understanding. Some decisions are formidable to make, but the alternatives also need to be viewed and taken into account.

Before we consider further, then, such matters as the apparently different kinds of reality with which we are faced—including subjective and objective reality and, from another viewpoint, the realities physical, moral and spiritual—we had better bring together briefly, as a basis for comparison, a few notes about the general scheme and pattern of existence. We have already referred to the subject, from time to time. We are likely, moreover, to find that, in every field of human existence into which we may look, the prototype of a general design is implemented in varying forms according to the particular circumstances.

A system, according to one of man's best friends, a truthful dictionary, is "a group of diverse units so combined by nature, or by art, as to form an integral whole and to function, operate or move, in unison, and, often, in obedience to some form of control."

In the prototype above mentioned, there is a governing principle that applies alike to the energies and the forces of a system and to the laws which govern the functioning of the system. All elements of the scheme and its operation are integrated by the principle in such manner as to be mutually sustaining in the achievement of an objective in common.

Ideally, the system, in whole, and, in part, would be so perfectly self-sustaining as to be, in itself, always both a means and an end. Actually, however, every imperfect system, in order to function for long, if at all, requires both a source and a purpose beyond itself.

In the design of existence there is finally one principle that unifies all others—that is, if there is to be a universe. It is a supreme principle. Without one unifying principle supreme there would be no real basis for such a thing as a universe.

Within such terms of reference, every dynamic system discernible in human life comprises a variety of circumstance and two mutually opposing forces that drive energetically one against the other. Rest and motion are resulting phenomena. A system of opposing forces implies an equilibrium between such forces as of a given point and moment.

The English word, principle, derives from the Latin *principium*, which, translated, means a beginning or a foundation. Accordingly, principle has the meaning of source, or origin, an ultimate basis, or cause. "Everything is inherent in the genesis."

The word, principle, is also taken to apply, in particular, on every plane of human thought. It applies, for instance, all the way from the mechanical principle of the sail and of the motive force of the steam engine, to the constitutional principle of a representative government and to religious principle. An economy, in its simplest terms, is any practical system in which means are adjusted to ends. There is a principle applicable to every kind of economy. For every true principle, there are corresponding ideas which are parts of the one great concept which we seek to identify as thought itself.

Principle naturally expresses itself in, and by, its own laws. This is a fact for us to view again when, further along in this chapter, we come to consider the respective characteristics of perfection and of imperfection.

And, meanwhile, in the scheme of the universe, what about the different forms of mind, or comparable apparatus, whereby to conform to the laws of existence, which we call also natural law? Within animate existence, up to and including man, there are various kinds of manifestations of a mental apparatus, comprising faculties for storing knowledge and wisdom, and for adding thereto, in regard to thought.

The "mental" apparatus of a plant, for instance, as also of borderline animal life, may be only a diffuse mechanism incapable of response to stimuli by the sensory means known to many of its more or less advanced relatives in the world around us. It evidences, nevertheless, its special brand, or mixture, of sensitivity and sensibility. In response to a particular scheme and pattern of life, the given mechanism manages to sustain and control a vital economy of its own, circumscribed as it may be.

From the lowest to the highest forms of animate existence —lowest to highest, as gauged arbitrarily in terms of mentality as discernible by man—there is evidence of a faculty to respond to the force of existence, an urge to conform to the laws of nature, for some good reason. There is evidence of instinct, up scale to intuition, and to conscience.

An essential difference between the animate spark and the inanimate object is that the inanimate being has no faculty of choice or, at least, appears to have no chosen purpose of its own, no pattern of growth nor clearly defined cycle of self-fulfillment.

Inanimate existence, as compared with the animate, has energy but no apparent choice of direction, no "free will." It lacks the force of an idea of its own choosing, by which to try to fulfill one mission as compared with another. Its nature is essentially good but it seems not to have a glimmer of the difference between right and wrong.

Sum, ergo cogito, I am, therefore, I think—but a mountain crag, for example, does not think and yet it is in being, it is amenable to nature's laws. Also, and with due respect to Monsieur Descartes, and to his *cogito, ergo sum*, the crag certainly does not exist because it thinks, if think be taken to have its usually accepted meaning. There must be something to be added, by way of context to one, or both, of the Latin statements in question. In reality, it would seem, the natural law is that every form in which existence is embodied, animate and inanimate, will conform to the general law according to a special pattern characteristic of the particular form itself. It is necessary to qualify both of the statements accordingly.

Man is human, therefore he thinks like a human being, not like an amoeba, or some other form of life. And—also by way of keeping ourselves in due perspective within the scheme of reality as a whole—could other forms of nature, animate or inanimate, exist on the Earth if there were no human being?

We still have a number of questions to examine under the present heading.

2.

Someone has pointed out, and it sounds like Dave Boone, that one nice thing about telling the truth is that you do not have to remember what you said.

It is a statement of the case that can often save a lot of time and trouble in regard to any aspect of a subject. It applies especially well to current matters, such as personal opinions and the circumstances of events. In addition, however, we are now interested in the changeless realities that also enter into the truth. We need to know more of the general relationships between reality and truth, including fact.

First, we could add to our recent notes concerning fact. There is a temporal element in the distinction between truth and fact. Arbitrarily, a fact is a truth in concrete form. Thus, it may be taken to include the nonphysical as well as the physical elements of any human event—which does not mean that everyone sees the facts alike.

There are different aspects of reality. Different kinds of reality appear to exist within reality as a whole. It is usual to recognize subjective reality as compared with objective, not that there would be a difference between the two for anyone possessing perfect knowledge and absolute wisdom.

Subjective reality is the truth as interpreted by a human mind. It is a mental interpretation of reality, of reality in whole and in part, as true or false. Subjectively, either a truth or a falsehood can seem real. Subjective reality varies from person to person, and may also vary personally, from subject to subject, in its measure of recognition of the truth.

The fact is there. The truth is there. The mental instrument for reception, interpretation and evaluation is there. The problem is to identify and to accept the fact and the truth, tangible and intangible, as real, subjectively.

There are many forces that can influence the character of subjective reality for a person, and in turn, for a community. Instinct and intuition; the nature of the ideal, innate or later acquired, as a criterion in the matter of a conscientious choice; education and other forms of personal experience, including prayer; unsupported imaginings and concepts that are mixtures of truth and falsehood; careful thinking and careless mistakes—these are among the influences that bear upon the shape of subjective reality for us.

I find at hand a letter from an uncle of mine, in which he quotes an old newspaper clipping that he had come across recently between the pages of one of his books.

"Political and social conceptions," the clipping reads, "alone can not create great individuals. The development is a solitary experience, as fresh and original in each instance as if it had never been achieved by another. The important part of every person's life is that which nobody else knows anything about. The musings of the mind, the feelings of the heart, the aspirations of the soul—these are the things that make or mar us."

Objective reality is generally considered to be the truth and the fact, as unbiased by a person's opinion, or by the ideals which he has currently accepted as true. Sometimes objective reality is defined, accordingly, not only as external, but also as entirely independent of the subjective. This may seem to be true in the abstract but the fact appears to be otherwise.

The recent age of materialism has confused objective reality with the physical and, in turn, with the whole truth. We have a habit of defining objective reality as solely physical and external, whereas there is another factor to be considered also, namely, the changeless ideal.

Objective reality is a form of the truth but, as far as human life be concerned, we can not well support an assumption that the objective is entirely independent of the subjective. For human beings, the two aspects of reality are interrelated and can be interacting.

Subjective reality influences human decision and human decision influences the objective trend of events. Again it takes the unifying principle and its laws to bring both the subjective and the objective into true perspective for us.

On the other hand, we can accept the idea that reality, as viewed objectively, can truly exist externally, and independently of man. The pine tree and the hemlock in the yard could be here even if there were none of us around to see them. In order that we may not take ourselves too seriously, but seriously enough, we are informed scientifically, by well-qualified students of the subject, that man is the recent arrival on the Earth. The pine tree and the hemlock are comparatively old-timers. They were here ages before man. Without the human being, other forms of nature could exist on the Earth.

It does not follow necessarily, if at all, however, that humanity of its own will—or, rather, the human being of his own will—can cease, in reality, to exist. Subjective and objective reality apply to concepts of the spiritual plane as well as of the moral and physical planes.

The truth is eternal as well as temporal. In a system of opposites, the imperfect implies the perfect. The perfect elements among the ingredients of the moral plane, the concepts of perfection, must be able to last forever in order to be perfect. "I believe in . . . the resurrection of the body and the life everlasting"—in the transcendence of temporal barriers by the human being.

Man is a part of the scheme and pattern of reality. His life, not in the abstract, but concretely, with its personal endowment and its particular events, is the one possession of which he can not finally divest himself. He has no choice about the actuality and the reality of his existence. His choice, we can reason accordingly, is only between perfect and imperfect existence.

The eternal question with which men are faced, ever personally, on the Earth is not "to be, or not to be." Men are parts of human existence whether they like it, or not. The question is not even to believe, or not to believe. In the scheme and pattern of reality, personal belief of one kind or the other is inescapable. The question is what to believe, and why, as a guide to what to do, and how.

Reality is made up of the truth in various forms, of the truth about existence, temporal and eternal.

3.

Subjective and objective reality are terms that apply systematically to the truth on every plane of human thinking, in every area of thought. They are classifications that apply to physical, moral and spiritual phenomena, one and all. They relate, for example, to the physical existence of our above-mentioned acquaintances, the pine and the hemlock. Likewise, moral issues can be viewed subjectively and objectively. They are terms and classifications that relate also to spiritual concepts of perfection.

We had already thought about the trees in the yard and

of how they could get along without us. But what about the realities of the moral and the spiritual forms of existence?

Right and wrong are the flags of the moral issue. They are the moral counterparts of good and evil, the factual counterparts that also are not always distinguishable one from the other because of the fallibility of human choice.

Good, and its opposite, qualitatively are of the spiritual plane absolute, we may say, but right and wrong are mixtures that are relative. And the moral issue is peculiarly human in that it involves the inevitable human choice. In a dynamic system, such as mankind's life on the Earth with its continual interplay of conflicting forces, a human being either exercises his faculty of choice, reaches a positive decision and acts accordingly, or the decision goes by default.

The decision goes by default and so, at best, plays more or less into the hand of chance, or, at worst, into the hands of a thoroughly organized opposition. In any case, a choice has been made, be the circumstances extenuating, or otherwise.

In an issue that involves right and wrong, a personal decision one way or the other is unavoidable as a matter of principle. It is denied to the individual, and consequently to the community, to stand aside blamelessly from the innate right and duty of taking sides in the moral issue. The rule is that the responsibility be rightly discharged, or the authority lost. The difficulties to be overcome can vary, as they do, and some seem beyond withstanding. Strong winds grow strong trees.

There is a paramount moral issue which we need to mention further, and with greatest care, before we proceed to view some of the realities in regard to the absolute. The issue involves the choice of the supreme principle of human life.

Earlier in these pages we have stated a general theory that human existence is a supremacy of good will, that good will, making use of spiritual and physical means, is the predominant force of human being. The principle of our theory is the principle of human life and of benevolent sovereignty which is otherwise known as the Christian principle.

A principle can be identified by its natural laws, and especially by its supreme law but, so far, we have not recorded explicitly the sovereign laws of the Christian principle. These are the two Great Commandments of the Christian faith:

"Thou shalt love the Lord thy God with all thy heart, and with all thy soul, and with all thy mind. This is the first and great Commandment. And the second is like unto it: Thou shalt love thy neighbor as thyself. On these two Commandments hang all the Law and the Prophets."

Tens of thousands of years ago, when man began to exercise a measure of control over fire and other physical manifestations of reality, he was probably awed. He was puzzled about the nature of the flame as his descendants have been puzzled, too. He must have been pleased, also, and encouraged by his accomplishments.

When man learned to transport supplies of water from place to place, the broadening circle of his activities led beyond the river bank into new territory, not only geographically but also morally. Through husbandry, man emerged from savagery into barbarism, testing ceaselessly, by his imagination and by actual experience, the bounds as well as the uses of natural law. His desires and his accepted beliefs, tempered by actual experiment, have led him forward into the realm of moral consciousness which we call civilization. There he now stands at the crossroads.

The choice is between a true imitation of the supreme

design of human existence, in which the law is that good
will always has the upper hand morally, and a setback of
proportions which can be imagined only too clearly.

4.

Of Valiant, when he came to the bank of the River of
Death, Bunyan tells us in "Pilgrim's Progress" that "he passed
over, and all the trumpets sounded for him on the other side."

But, in advance of actual eternity there is no matter-of-
fact answer, yes or no, about the hereafter. Faith and the
unknown are as much parts of the scheme of human life on
Earth as are doubt and reason, and the known. Man lives
on the Earth in a context of here and now, and, in this world,
at least, human thought is free to desire but not always to
achieve the desire. Human thought is free of the barriers of
space and time. In the world, what man can imagine, he can
do—but only step by step, within the bounds of nature's laws.

Again we are brought face to face with the need for the
ideal of absolute perfection to be a real ideal. Such a reality
is necessary, if the scheme and pattern of existence is to be
so reliable as to justify loyalty, hopefulness and excellence
of performance on the part of the members of a human community. It is in keeping with such need that our initial hypothesis has taken for granted that thoughts, in almost endless
variety, are waiting to be discovered, or revealed, as parts
of the great and perfect concept of existence.

There are a number of characteristics of a state of perfection that can be reasonably imagined, if not actually seen,
characteristics of an abstract, or an impersonal, nature, as
compared with the personal attributes of the ideal of perfection. There is, for example, our erstwhile finding that per-

fection, in order to be absolute, has to be always so. Perfect existence is, by very definition, eternal.

In a state of perfection, the truths and facts that we encounter in daily life would endure forever. On the contrary, there would be no place for the temporal imperfections and falsehoods which can now seem real enough, subjectively. They would turn out to be against the law. Under perfect conditions, the truths of subjective reality would coincide with those of the objective, the purpose of the infinite could be reconciled in terms of the finite—and the right answers would come out even.

In a perfect state of affairs, absolute free will, or complete freedom of human choice, would coincide with omniscience, or full knowledge and wisdom. Therein, it would be entirely clear that, in final justice, the reward of true loyalty and obedience to the laws of existence would be so great that, even were there no punishment in the offing for the law breaker, there could be ultimately no reasonable, nor right, choice for man but to desire to live forever.

For the human being, however, the live and personal attributes of perfection constitute the most important element of all. For mankind, there is nothing in the world really to take the place of personal regard and affection, nothing in the universe as we now know it. Man is encouraged to believe that such is the truth—and we reason respectfully, as well as searchingly, on the thought—because the Deity requires Himself to be personified in order to be loved. It is not in human nature to "love" abstractions.

God is the name by which we, of the English tongue, have come to think and speak of perfect existence, a Being Perfect in Person, perfect in personal and also impersonal relationships. God is the actual as well as potential source of almighty power and goodness. He has revealed Himself and His nature to the human mind in many ways.

One of the ways is through His laws. There is one more observation now to be made, as bearing specifically on our theory. Under the laws of the design and system of reality, the force of existence dominates the opposition thereto. With all its justice and mercy, and in all its power and glory, the absolute perfection of the Supreme Being, in order to be so, must be able, of itself, to overcome imperfection, not only at first sign, but also eternally.

There is a reflection of the supreme principle in Ibsen's idea that "the strongest man on earth is he who stands most alone," more than a little reflection, be the idea in, or out of, due context. In the scheme and pattern of reality, perfect existence is both a means and an end in the fulfillment of the great concept of itself.

CHAPTER FIVE

Dialectical Materialism

HEGEL, one of the great philosophers of 19th century Europe—Georg Wilhelm Friedrich Hegel (1770-1831)—was born at Stuttgart, into a German family of moderately comfortable circumstances. His father was a minor government official. Educated in theology, the atmosphere in which Hegel spent almost his entire career was one of higher learning.

He was a tutor in Frankfort-on-the-Main and in Switzerland, a professor at Jena and at Heidelberg, the rector of a school at Nuremberg. It is also noteworthy, by way of prologue, that these formative years of his were among those of Napoleon's ascendancy in Europe. It was at the University of Berlin that Hegel came into prominence. In 1818, he went there as a professor and made Berlin his home until the end of his days.

Early in his career, Hegel began to develop his own system of philosophy. Two different influences were greatly upon him, namely, his education in theology and, second, the mechanistic view of human life which had been gaining sway in the popular imagination during the centuries which had followed the times of Francis Bacon and Descartes.

Hegel wrote books on such deeply related subjects as ethics, aesthetics, religion, philosophy and history. His many and varied interests and ideas, original and otherwise, were

at last brought together and set forth in his unified philosophy. He became famous for the lectures in which he elaborated the philosophical system propounded in his writings.

According to Hegelian philosophy, the universe developed by a self-creating plan. The world process is the absolute, an "absolute" which does not, however, transcend the
realm of time and space, but which exists through and in
such terms. His absolute ideal envisaged a "world-soul" that
develops logically out of, and is known through, dialectic—
or, if you do not object to pleonasm, through dialectical
logic.

Dialectic, by definition, turns out to be either logic, in
general, or, in another sense, a specific theory, or mode, of
reasoning. Plato used a dialectical method in the form of
questions and answers. The word comes from two Greek
roots which join to mean "speak between." For our present
purpose, a dialectic is a logical sequence.

According to Hegel's dialectical logic, one idea or concept
(thesis) is bound always to generate its opposite (antithesis),
and the interplay of these two concepts leads to a new concept (synthesis). The synthesis, in turn, represents a concept
(thesis) and the dialectic continues, more or less indefinitely,
from thesis to antithesis to synthesis. It seemed as simple, or as
cut and dried, as that, and Hegel applied his theory, as a universal law, to various kinds of phenomena.

For example, the self-creating plan of the universe proceeds from astral bodies to the world, from the mineral kingdom to the animal kingdom, and so on and on. Man's activities
lead to property and property to law. Law leads to ethics.

A thesis of human interdependence raises an antithesis of
individual freedom, and these two lead to a synthesis in the
form of the State, a totality above all individuals. Since the
State is a unit, he reasoned, its highest development is rule

by monarchy. The State is the embodiment of Hegel's "absolute" ideal, the world-soul. In his study of history, he reviewed the stories of States that had held sway over less powerful peoples "until a higher representative of the absolute evolves."

Hegel taught that, in religion, man's concept moved from a worship of nature, through a series of stages of dialectical logic, to Christianity, in which Christ represents the union of God and man, of spirit and matter. He opined that philosophy goes beyond religion, because philosophy enables man to comprehend the absolute.

This was all very intriguing, not to say well, and Hegelian philosophy was received with open arms by, among others, the socialist elements of those days. The influence of Hegel's thinking seems to have been profound in Europe, at various levels of human society. And there are several parts of his philosophy that are of special interest, also, in connection with the thinking that is now being set forth elsewhere herein.

First, it may be noted that Hegel's "absolute" is a *world* process. He does not pry beyond a materially self-creating plan. Like Descartes, Hegel does not explicitly inquire into the nature of thought itself, although he apparently accepts Descartes' pronouncement, *"cogito, ergo sum."*

Second, it is significant that Hegel's thesis and antithesis are, in fact, not absolute opposites at all. The principle, or source, is not absolute although he calls it so. The final source is not sought. His opposites are not mutually exclusive. There is, illogically enough, room for compromise of the principle itself in the system that is supposed to be governed by the principle.

In this connection, we may well pause to reason for ourselves that such departure from absolute principle can but lead, at last, to a descending scale of effectiveness of the principle—as witness the rise and fall of empire. And such departure, if permitted to continue, can finally lead but to the obliteration of the system that is self-defeating in terms of disloyalty and disobedience to the source from which the system sprang.

There is a confusion, in Hegel's dialectical logic, between the concrete circumstance and the abstract ideal. There is no changeless, distinct and ever reliable criterion in his logic, by which to choose among alternatives in aim and in course of action.

And, particularly important from the standpoint of human progress, the impact of deliberate choice, of conscientious individual effort upon a series of events, is not taken into final account by Hegel. His philosophy, for all of its acceptance and explanation of religious thought, looks at this distance to be essentially a concept of mechanistic cause and effect in a world of—to use a modern term—pragmatism.

Incidentally, it seems unfortunate to restrict the application of the term pragmatism to things material. Pragmatism means a school of thought in which practical results are considered the real criteria for truth. The idea should not be confined to the workings of physical nature. It is a term that could be applied equally well to systems of all planes of existence, including the moral and the spiritual. So much for a mild digression to investigate a definition on the spot.

Trier, known also to us as Treves, is a beautiful old German city that looks through early landmarks to its Roman days of pre-eminence. In 1818, the same year that Hegel went to a professorship at Berlin, Karl Marx was born in Trier. The seeds of Hegelian philosophy were to fall in fateful soil, indeed, with the birth of the man who later was to say, with utmost logic mechanistically, "The policy of communism is changeless. Its methods, its tactics, its manoeuvers may change. But the polar star of communist policy—world domination—is a fixed star."

2.

Karl Heinrich Marx came of a well-to-do Jewish family. His parents are recorded as having gone over to Christianity, as Protestants, when Karl was little more than an infant. His father was a jurist, and Karl grew up to study law, at Bonn and later at Berlin. It was not long, however, before he became more interested in philosophy than in law, and especially interested in the Hegelian dialectic.

The French Revolution, with its violent disillusionment about mediaeval teachings, its hatred of intrenched monarchial and religious authority and with its worship of man's reason, was still fresh in the peoples' minds, as was also the fall of Napoleon. The pendulum was swinging from one extreme toward the other. It was a revolutionary age in various parts of Europe and America, although the causes and the actual reasons for the different conflicts were not all the same.

Marx had been old enough in 1830 to be impressed by the talk about the European uprisings of that year. By the time he came of age, his political views had moved to the extreme left.

The so-called liberal newspaper, of which he had become editor, after further studies leading to a Ph.D. at Jena in 1842, was suppressed by the government in the Rhineland in 1843. Marx betook himself to Paris where, in 1844, he began his lifelong association with Friedrich Engels, whose origin and background should also be inquired into briefly in a moment.

During Europe's revolutionary years of 1848 and 1849, Marx spent some time again in Germany. When such activities, by then known as communist, had failed in their current purposes in Germany, he went, with his wife and children, to London, where he resided the remainder of his life. Marx's personal life and its paradoxes are beyond our present scope, but it has bearing on his accomplishments to point out his dedication to the communist concept in the face of serious obstacles.

Among other of his problems, Marx had little financial means of his own. During part of the London years, years that were eager, on both sides of the Atlantic, in regard to political panaceas, he was a correspondent of a New York newspaper. The income from the articles which he furnished to Horace Greeley's *Tribune* helped toward the support of his family and himself, while he spent his time, day in and day out, at the British Museum writing his most famous work, *Das Kapital*.

The first of the three volumes of the massive "Capital," to use the English title, was published in 1867. Karl Marx died in 1883. Volumes II and III of *Das Kapital* were edited by Friedrich Engels and published in the period from 1885 to 1894. English translations of the entire work from the original German were not made until the beginning of the present century, that is, from 1901 to 1909.

Friedrich Engels (1820-1895) was the son of a wealthy textile manufacturer. The family was German but its business interests included a factory near Manchester in England. There Engels had gone to work as a young man, and was shocked by the abuses of the industrial revolution then under way.

It was while passing through Paris, rather than in residing

there, that Engels had met Karl Marx, of whom from then on Engels was an active and independently effective associate. From 1845 to 1850, Engels was busy in Germany, France and Belgium organizing revolutionary movements. He made his home permanently in England, beginning in 1848. Engels was a successful businessman and from his income aided Marx to devote the latter's life largely to research and to writing.

So much by way of brief biography and a few comments in regard to three of the 19th century's thinkers, Hegel, Marx and Engels, who, either knowingly or unknowingly, directly or indirectly, contributed by their words and deeds, as well as by their ideas, to the advancement, not only of the socialist, but also of the communist cause.

It had been the expressed opinion of Marx, among others, that the seeds of the extreme socialism known as communism would most likely take root, first of all, in Germany. He was wrong in this prognostication.

It was in the political soil of the vast areas and different peoples which went to form the Russian Empire that the seeds of communism were to take hold and begin their predatory growth. The growth was to be in the form of the political implementation of the atheistic concept that impersonal, physical power, vested systematically in the sovereign state, is the supreme force in the human universe.

There is a fourth name, then, to add, particularly to our list in connection with communism's rise to political power. It is the name of Lenin, the master mind of communism's Russian venture and one of the most astute and most successful revolutionists of all times.

Before tackling Lenin, however, there are some further points to consider about Karl Marx, after which it would also be useful, as a matter of perspective, to glance backward through history to at least a few milestones in the growth of sovereign power in Russia, prior to the advent of Soviet rule.

3.

Hegel's dialectical logic was made to order for Marx's keen intellect, prejudiced as it already was by the "mechanical view" of human life. Marx saw without delay the inherent weakness of the Hegelian dialectic, with its fictitious "absolute," as a philosophy whereby to reconcile the material with the divine. Instead, Marx made a really absolute choice between God and man in the matter of supremacy. There is no God, said Marx. The supreme element in human affairs is the physical. In the final analysis, it is physical needs and physical force that determine man's destiny.

Marx held tacitly to the Hegelian concept of thesis, antithesis and synthesis, but developed his own powerful theory of economic change and class conflict, that is known as Marxism. His theory and doctrine are also called "dialectical materialism" or "materialistic determinism."

In 1848, at the request of a conference of communists, held in London the preceding year, Marx and Engels published the now famous *Communist Manifesto*. This is a document, say, of some thirty-five medium-sized, printed pages, or well over 10,000 words. The copy which I have for reference purposes has an introduction of about seven pages by Engels, as of 1888.

The *Manifesto*, itself, is a rambling train of extreme ideas, full of vague and fearful intimations of power and hatred that, judged by common sense, are as hard to grasp as a snake. At the same time, it is to be recognized as a sincere protest against some of the social abuses of the 1840's that now are only too clearly recognized, and that have been mostly overcome long ago in, and by, the industrial West. Meanwhile, the venom of the *Communist Manifesto* has had over a hundred years in which to spread methodically throughout the world.

The *Manifesto* is a document to be read in full and to be considered as a whole, rather than by means of extracting a sentence here and there. Out of context, its paragraphs are likely to lose their full flavor.

Among other things, however, the words of the *Manifesto* boil down, not only to a theme of socialist and communist conquest of supreme political power by any means whatsoever, but also to a declaration of such aims and purposes as the negation of religious beliefs and of morality and to the abolition of private property, of family institutions, and of love of country. There is an intent to create an awesome fear. "A spectre is haunting Europe—the spectre of Communism" is the way the *Manifesto* begins.

In his preface of 1888 to the *Communist Manifesto* of 1848 —atheism having been assumed explicitly by him as part of the hypothesis—Engels has the following to say in regard to the original proposition of communism and Marx's responsibility therefor:

"The *Manifesto* being our joint production, I consider myself bound to state that the fundamental proposition which formed its nucleus, belongs to Marx. That proposition is: That in every historical epoch, the prevailing mode of economic production and exchange and the social organization necessarily following from it, form the basis upon which it is built up, and from which alone can be explained, the political and intellectual history of that epoch; that consequently the whole history of mankind (since the dissolution of primitive tribal society, holding land in common ownership) has been a history of class struggles, contests between exploiting and exploited, ruling and oppressed classes; that the history of these class struggles forms a series of evolutions in which, nowadays, a stage has been reached where the exploited and oppressed class—the proletariat—cannot attain its emancipation from the exploiting and ruling class—the bourgeoisie—without at the same time, and once and for all, emancipating society at large from all exploitations, oppressions, class distinctions and class struggles."

Nathaniel Hawthorne happens, in this instance, to run a poor second in length of sentence but, as a matter of real importance, the above statement is, unfortunately, no casual affair. Its substance, in the face of confused opponents, has already led to swift territorial conquest on an unprecedented scale. The conquest will continue, we can reason, if it be within the bounds of nature's laws. Otherwise, we can be sure that there will be a day of reckoning in just proportion to the mistakes that have been made all around.

"What are you fighting for?" the native Frenchman, turned Island planter, asks the American naval captain in the post-World War II musical play, "South Pacific." The question is a real one. Essentially, it is always more important to know what we are fighting for than what we are fighting against. In order to avoid big mistakes, in order to gain and always to hold the upper hand in a good cause, it is necessary to know what principle above all we are fighting for, to know why as well as how the principle works.

To get back to the *Manifesto*, it is, as a final thought for now, an illuminating experience to compare the atheism of the communist document with the American Declaration of Independence and its worshipful belief in a Divine Providence. Both of these pronouncements are revolutionary in purpose but, between the respective propositions of the two, there is all the difference in this world of ours, namely, the difference between opposite concepts of the final source of human power.

One world, physically? One world, spiritually? One principle in terms of which to balance the two in the universe? The happy medium is in terms of one principle, not of one world.

Man-made rule is never absolutely perfect. Furthermore, as of collateral interest, the political concept of revolution, in itself, is, accordingly, neither good nor evil. It depends, in principle, on why the revolution is taking place, on what its ideals and purposes are, on how the rules of morality are observed, as to whether one revolution is right and another one wrong.

And there is no substitute for the initiative in any cause on earth. Karl Marx was out to seize the initiative for communism.

4.

The Slav tribes bordering on Scandinavia, history tells us, were first consolidated under Rurik, leader of the Russ, who established his seat of power at Novgorod, A.D. 862. His successors moved toward the Black Sea and ruled from Kiev, as the Grand Dukes of Kiev, and then as the Grand Dukes of Vladimir. The sovereign line at Kiev was converted to the Christian faith of the Eastern church toward the end of the 10th century.

Novgorod, beginning in the 12th century, was so much left to its own devices that it achieved political independence and, known as Great Novgorod, extended its sovereignty over colonies in adjacent territories, before coming under Russian rule again, some three hundred years later. Located on the trade routes between Europe and Asia, the Baltic, the

Volga River and the Caspian Sea, it achieved wealth and commercial greatness, including membership in the Hanseatic League. Rich and comparatively unprotected against the force of arms, Great Novgorod—and "great" has a now archaic meaning of united in friendship—was an easy prize to violence, when the situation was ripe. Sovereignty over its affairs was lost to its physically stronger neighbor to the south.

Under the leadership of a grandson of Genghis Khan in the course of the 13th century, Asiatic invaders, Mongolian and other—known as the Golden Horde and also, in general, as Tartars—overran Russia, Novgorod excepted, and established the capital of their rule at Sarai, on the Volga near the site of modern Stalingrad. For some two hundred years, they exacted tribute from among the feudal principalities in Russia that were struggling also among themselves for power.

Against such background, the principality of Moscow, founded about 1295, rose gradually to a place of dominance. The Grand Dukes of Vladimir were followed by the Muscovy dynasty, which ruled from Moscow, as the name implies. The Grand Duke of Muscovy, in the person of Ivan IV, was crowned "Czar of All the Russias" in 1547. His contemporaries in Western Europe include, among others, the Emperor Charles V of the Holy Roman Empire, King Francis I of France, and King Henry VIII of England.

The Muscovy dynasty was succeeded in 1613 by the Romanov. Czar Peter I, the Great, (1682-1725), built a new capital at Saint Petersburg, now Leningrad, to which he transferred the seat of imperial government. Czar Alexander I of the Romanov line was the ally, and afterwards the opponent, of Napoleon in the early 19th century.

Czar Nicholas II, who had inherited the imperial throne in 1894, ruled until he was forced to abdicate in March, 1917. He and his rule were destroyed as a result of many factors that added up to an ineffectual administration, often lacking in benevolence, and to Russian military defeats during World War I.

Most of the comparatively powerful nations of the world, during the centuries that followed the discovery of America, were busy with wars among themselves, and with struggles for territory and power in various parts of the New World, India and Africa. There resulted practically a political vacuum in the vast region that stretches from the Ural mountains, north of the Himalayas and China, to the Pacific Ocean. Russian sovereignty was extended eastward accordingly, and with a vitality that carried Russian dominion for a while, as as far as the present Alaskan Territory of the United States.

The outline in the above paragraphs does not pretend to be more than a few dates of Russian history linked together mostly by reference to successive lines of hereditary rulers. The milestones of the Kremlin's bid for universal power are still in actual view. The outline is partly for purposes of comparison chronologically with developments elsewhere in the world, partly to set off the fact that the record of Russian sovereignty is largely one of autocratic rule.

For all of its frequent vigor and long established position, the ruling element of the empire was not sustained and strengthened systematically by the body politic. Actually, religion and politics remained mostly in separate compartments. Only the feeble beginning of a representative assembly, the Duma, had made its appearance at the turn of the 20th century. The dynamic peoples of Russia were not prepared, either by experience or organization, to entertain self-government when the Czar fell.

Autocratic rule as a temporary measure in an emergency may well be a moral necessity, but only as rightful exception and not as a fixed habit of government. As a matter of principle, the ideal is a minimum of interference with the exercise of individual, human choice within a framework of just law.

Anyhow, Lenin was in Switzerland in 1917, and ready for his political opportunity when it arrived.

5.

Vladimir Ilyich Ulyanov (1870-1924)—he later took the name of V. I. Lenin and is often referred to also, for some obscure reason, as Nicolai Lenin—was born in Simbirsk, a city of Tartary, on the Volga River some four hundred miles southeast of Moscow. Simbirsk has, in the course of communism, been renamed Ulyanovsk in Lenin's honor.

The future Lenin was the son of a school official of some local importance, and, as did also Hegel and Marx, the young Ulyanov set out at first to study law. He went to the University of Kazan, in Tartary, for that purpose, and later to Saint Petersburg, but this phase of his career was cut short by his revolutionary aims and activities. His leanings in that direction were intensified, at this time, by the execution of his older brother, for having taken part in a plot against the life of Czar Alexander III, the father and imperial predecessor of Nicholas II.

Giving up his legal practice, Lenin devoted his attention almost undividedly to the study of Marxism and to revolutionary propaganda, especially among the workers of Saint Petersburg. He was there imprisoned for his pains and also ended up in Siberia for a while. Upon his release and departure for more congenial climes outside Russia, he became increasingly influential in the exiled Russian Social Democratic Party. When the party split into two, namely, the Mensheviks, or moderates, and the Bolsheviks, or radicals, Lenin headed the latter party.

On the Eastern front in 1917, Russian resistance to the Germans was collapsing. Apparently, in order to make doubly sure in that regard, safe transit was granted by the German Command to Lenin and to some of his associates—all presumably useful revolutionists to turn loose against the pro-Allied, Czarist government—to go from Switzerland, through Germany, to Russia.

The Provisional Government, formed in Russia upon the overthrow of the Czar in March, 1917, was the Menshevik government under Prince Lvov and later under Kerensky. The regime was weakening, Lenin found, upon his arrival in his homeland. In November, 1917, the Bolsheviks seized the sovereign power from the moderates. Lenin became Chairman of the Council of People's Commissars and virtual dictator in the former Russian Empire, from then until his death in 1924. Moscow again became the seat of Russian government with the mediaeval citadel, the Kremlin, as the inner sanctum and the world symbol of the godless State.

What manner of human being is this, the leader whose body is enshrined, open to the view of the presumably faithful, as well as curious, in his tomb on the Red Square in Moscow, the leader for whom cities have been named and whose followers talk about the dignity of man?

Lenin was the great organizer politically of the Soviet Socialist Union. It was he, above all, who had the concept in the precarious days of budding communism, that revolution should be preceded by a strongly organized political party, a hard core of ideological strength as an essential nucleus of power within the Communist State. It was Lenin who elaborated and began to implement the concept of "unconditional surrender" of the individual to the "central will."

He carried forward Marx's theory of dialectical materialism to the logical conclusion of the all-powerful State. He made use of various opportunities to identify such State with the interests of Russian nationalism. He began to exploit the truly inspired patriotism of the Russian peoples—heretofore traditional friends of the American Republic—as a means of strengthening the hold of the communist regime on the populace.

And, in addition to his deeds, here are some of the thoughts that Lenin has left behind in his written words:

"Our Communist world revolution may occupy years or even decades. There will occur, nay, must occur, ebbs and flows in the revolutionary tide."

"We must with all our heart—or, better, *without* a heart—but calculatingly, favor concessions now and then."

"Any technique, from giving a man poison to giving a diplomatic reception, must be carefully thought out."

"Let us turn toward Asia. We will reach the West by way of the East."

"The day will come when we will force the United States to spend itself into destruction."

CHAPTER SIX

Of Ergs, Dynes and Effort

ALL knowledge and wisdom in regard to the physical is actually or potentially a means of valuable information in other fields of human interest and concern. Every mathematical and physical principle, among others, suggests the existence of a counterpart.

There seems to be a countless number of camparisons to be made between phenomena of the contrasting planes of thought as well as between those of one and the same plane. In this chapter we are dealing especially with comparisons in the form of analogy, and are keeping in mind, it is hoped, that findings by such a method are subject to verification by well-principled and carefully executed experiment, or in other truly acceptable ways.

Analogy, it is to be noted as another reminder, does not mean an all-around likeness. Analogy is a matter of resemblance, in quality, or in function.

For instance, any and all political ideals of a general nature —ideals such as freedom and peace, security and plenty, for each and every good member of the community—are not exactly the same aims in our current affairs, but they are analogous in that they are of like quality, one with the other.

And, functionally, an analogy is a resemblance from the standpoint of respective relationships. Inanimate existence is to the mathematical and physical sciences as animate existence is to biological science. There is an analogy between the cycles of different forms of life. As among the various parts of an entity, or whole, there are analogies of design and of operation.

As discernible on the moral plane of our daily lives, physical and spiritual laws are analogous laws of nature. The respective coordinate systems of the physical and the spiritual do not move uniformly in relation to each other, but are reconciled by a principle common to both.

In pursuing an idea of this kind, there are, to begin with, a few related words that may be troublesome, even within a physical framework alone, unless their meanings be distinguished explicitly one from the other. For instance, there are the terms energy, work, force and power.

In physics, *energy* is the capacity for performing work. Some of us are likely also to associate the term "energy" with a corresponding flow, or current, and not the transmission of energy from one particle of matter to another. But an energy, or energy in varying degree, pertains essentially to respective units of mass, or other pieces of matter, and is not a fluid, nor a unit of flow.

There is a sequence of events. Analogously, there can be said to be a current of energy. There is a wave theory as well as a corpuscular theory of light. Analogies and currents aside, however, energy is primarily the relative capacity of a given unit, or other particle of matter, for performing work —and this fact holds good with respect to an atom as well as for any other piece of material substance.

A particle of matter—or, likewise, any material body—may have energy, either due to the motion of the particle, or due to the position of the particle with reference to other particles. These are the two general classifications of causation

in respect to physical energy with which we are now concerned.

Energy due to motion is known as kinetic energy. Energy
due to position is known as potential energy. And, be it a
time of peace or war between variously armored and differ-
ently located nations, energy may be transmitted from one
particle of matter to another in different forms and by a
number of processes. For example, there are mechanical,
thermal, chemical, and electric processes by which, singly or
jointly, to transmit energy in corresponding forms.

To quote Louis MacNeice, in the mechanistic vein—

> "Upon the deck they take beef-tea
> Who are so free, so free, so free.
> But down the ladder in the engine-room
> (Doom, doom, doom, doom)
> The great cranks rise and fall, repeat,
> The great cranks plod with their Assyrian feet
> To match the monotonous energy of the sea."

Taking high velocities into account with respect to material particles, there is another scientific finding for us to examine also, for us to look into more fully in due course. It is a
finding of comparatively recent years and, again, one which
we have already had occasion to mention. It can now be noted
to the effect that energy and mass are essentially the same,
that physical energy and mass, or matter, turn out to be different forms of the same substance, as do also the magnetic
field and the electric, in relation to each other.

Moreover, it develops that there is a conservation of energy
within the system of physical nature and that there is a natural law accordingly. In physics, if a system be not acted upon

by another—Iron Curtain, or no—the sum of potential and kinetic energies within the system remains constant, be internal transformations what they will.

There is a close relationship between work and energy. As already noted in passing, it is an axiom that energy is present wherever work is accomplished.

Work is defined, in the impersonal terms of physics—lacking, that is, the ingredients of human choice and human effort—as the accomplishment of motion, or of a change of motion, against the action of a force tending to resist such accomplishment.

In mechanics, work is the transference of energy by a process involving motion in the form of the displacement, or change of location, of the point of application of a force. If the displacement be in the same direction as that of the force, work is done by the force. If the displacement be in a direction opposite to that of the force, work is done on, or against, the force. In either event, two mutually opposing forces— and action and reaction—are implied.

Within our present terms of reference, energy can be taken to be the sum and total of actual work, and all that can arise from work, and all that can be converted into work. It is exhausting even to think about it.

Force, on the other hand, is causative. It has to do with origin, or source, and also with impact.

Force may be defined as any cause that tends to, or does, produce, stop or change the motion of a point of space, or, say, the motion of a mass or body. By the same token, a force is an agent by which resistance is overcome. Again, forces tending in opposite directions are implied.

In regard to the respective measurements of physical energy and force, or, at least, regarding arbitrary yardsticks, or standards of measurement, it is not difficult, for once, to be exact—more exact, if not more realistic, than in an appraisal of conscientious effort.

The *erg* (from the Greek *ergon*, work) is a standard unit of energy, being the work done when, under the influence of one dyne, the point of application of the force moves the distance of one centimeter in the same direction as the direction of the force.

The *dyne* (from the Greek *dynamis*, power) is a standard unit of force, being such force that, under its influence, a particle of which the mass is one gram, would experience, during each second, an acceleration of one centimeter per second. Indeed, this is something definite to be kept in mind not only by the engineers, with their dynamos and dynamite, but also by the individual with an admittedly dynamic personality.

More to the point-in-general of the foregoing, there is, thus, a real and useful difference between the respective meanings of physical energy and physical force, terms which are loosely used interchangeably more often than not.

Also, there are practical distinctions to be made between the two words, not only with respect to so-called purely physical phenomena, but also in regard to forces and energies that comprise human effort on the moral plane. Concerning human effort, for instance, an energetic nation may be too confused to be forceful, a forceful person may not be always energetic.

In the same group of words that includes energy, work, and force, there is also to be found the word *power*.

Mechanically, power is any form of energy—steam, electric, atomic, or other—available for doing any kind of work as distinguished from power by hand. But, by and large, in everyday conversation, power has a wider application of meaning than any other of the terms in the group.

It could even be that power has a tendency to become a special haven for vague meanings, and a vague idea is quite a different thing from a general concept. A general concept may be the hope of the world and, at the same time, the despair of the worldly perfectionist, but whatever else it may be, a truly general concept is not vague. It has the clarity, brevity and exactness of a natural law.

Meanwhile, among the various physical principles, or laws, and their functionings, we might choose two or three that seem to lend themselves to the purpose of our inquiry at this point, namely, to analogy with moral and spiritual principle and law.

Suppose we limit ourselves to the following choices and consider each, respectively, in the next three sections of this chapter: first, mechanical powers, so-called, which lead us to imagine the existence of counterparts in fields such as propaganda and salesmanship, not to mention also education and advertising; then, the behavior of one electron as compared with the behavior of another; and, last, physical transformation of mass and energy, as related to acceleration.

2.

According to usually accepted classification, there are six "mechanical powers." These relatively simple and basic devices represent discoveries of mechanical principles which have marked man's emergence from a state of savagery and have aided his advance toward civilization, especially in the sense of an advance scientifically.

These devices serve a purpose of increasing power at the expense of speed, or vice versa, or of changing the direction of motion.

Five of the six powers, comprising the lever and the four

derivatives of the lever, are as follows: the lever itself, the balance, the wheel and axle, the pulley and the funicular machine. The last named is best known, perhaps, in the form of funicular railways on steep grades, but it also includes the bow string and the ship's sail. The sixth of the powers is the inclined plane. The wedge and the screw are forms of the inclined plane.

In order to function, each and every one of these devices needs a motivating force outside of its own self. Each also requires an outside point of application of the resultant power.

If the two foregoing statements in regard to physical phenomena be true in general principle, it points to the natural law which we have already had occasion to mention, concerning the changeless sum and total of different forms of physical energy within an isolated system.

Within the bounds of physical nature, there is continually an overall conservation of energy. There arises, accordingly, the question, and the implication, of a conservation of energy within the bounds of all creation, which we can also think of as being nature, as a whole. The open question has to do with original and final form. Once in existence, always in existence—subject to the will of the Creator.

3.

An electron is the elementary charge, or unit, of what is arbitrarily called negative electricity. A beam of electrons is directed toward one pinhole in a cardboard which is placed in front of a photographic plate. Light and dark concentric circles are recorded on the plate.

But put a second pinhole near the first, and the result on the plate is, surprisingly enough, not two sets of concentric circles, but one set of parallel, dark and light stripes.

The repetition of the experiment over and over again, the record tells us, leads to a conclusion within the framework of the quantum theory, a theory already noted on an earlier page. The conclusion is that it is possible to predict the general result of the action of millions of electrons directed toward the two pinholes, but not to foretell the behavior of an individual electron.

One and more than one. The dual rôle of the individual. The individual acting alone and, at the same time, in relation to other individuals as inseparable parts of the whole.

4.

There are natural laws of limited and of general applicability, respectively, in physical nature. For example, there is the general law that has been found as a direct consequence of the development of the theory of Relativity. It is the law that is represented by the now famous Einsteinian equation, to the effect that energy equals mass times the square of the velocity of light, $E=mc^2$.

This equation is of so much significance, philosophically as well as scientifically, that it deserves particularly careful attention in our present calculations. It links, for instance, into the discoveries of Lord Rutherford (1871-1937) and his splitting of the atom. It shatters the ideal that perfection is to be found, accidentally or otherwise, in physical terms.

Many of the findings of classical physics from the ancient days to the times of Sir Isaac Newton, the great English physicist and philosopher, who lived from 1642 to 1727, were carried forward by the latter and reduced by him to simple statements of theory and of proven fact in the form of natural law. For instance, he advanced theories of light and color and formulated laws of gravitation and laws of motion.

Every particle in the universe attracts every other particle directly as the product of the masses, and indirectly as the square of the distance between the two particles. Thus reads the Newtonian law of gravitation and, within its terms of reference, it is the truth.

The law in question allows for mass and distance, however, but not for time. It turned out finally that it was not a general law, a law of physical nature as a whole. It proved impossible to explain electric and optical phenomena, for example, on a basis simply of constant forces acting between changeless objects. Observers in two aircraft which are airborne get a different view of each other, relatively, than an observer on the ground would get of either, or both, of the aircraft. As in many of life's calculations and evaluations, much actually depends on the point of view as well as on the yardstick.

And the Newtonian law does not allow for acceleration. Gravitational pull is not a constant for all degrees of acceleration.

Coördinates are any of two, or more, magnitudes or factors, that are of equal importance with one another in determining a position, or positions, within a given frame of reference. Physical nature is a system of coördinates. So is the human universe. With reference to the physical domain, coördinates may vary in kind from, say, the simple spatial coördinates on a map, to magnitudes such as mass and velocity in the dynamic systems of space and time.

As compared with the law of gravitation, a more inclusive law was needed, a law that would apply in general to physical phenomena, a law that would embrace all physical coördinate systems—that is, including systems moving non-uniformly as well as uniformly in relation to each other. A big step forward has been taken in response to the need.

Centuries of human thought and experience, of imagination, observation and scientific experiment—not least during the last seventy years or so—have culminated in our day in the advancement and the practical application of the General Theory of Relativity.

In Relativity, neither time nor space is absolute. Physical reality is conceived in terms of the "event." In the event, space and time are not viewed separately but are taken to be fused, as of a given point of space and corresponding moment. Events of solely physical reality are viewed as forming a space-time continuum which, we may say, is analogous to a sequence of human events. The case in favor of the concept of "here and now," as a natural center of equilibrium for human effort in aim and act, is strengthened by this view of reality.

In Relativity, neither mass nor energy is absolute. And, by-passing a technical problem like critical mass, we can note a little more specifically that, at speeds expressed in powers of the velocity of light, the mass of an object—of an atom, for example—can be transformed into energy.

In the final analysis, the science of physics deals with energy, or the equivalent of energy in terms of the ability to accomplish motion against resistance, which is another word for opposition. It does not deal ultimately with physical objects, or mass; $m = \dfrac{E}{c^2}$.

All motion, all work resulting from any force in the space-time continuum of the physical realm is relative. All physical forces, all energy and mass in motion, tend automatically to reach an equilibrium, but only a temporary and uneasy equilibrium.

The direction of moment-to-moment change of location, as between consecutive points of equilibrium, depends on the relative strengths of the forces entering into the equilibrium.

The direction depends, from one moment to the next, upon which of the opposing forces has the upper hand.

All material objects tend to wear out. There is no permanent rest, nor perpetual motion, within a physical system. Change is continual in every material circumstance.

Philosophically, there is no longer to be found, in the scheme and pattern of the physical nature, a basis for achieving therein alone, the absolute perfection which, in a system of opposites, is implied throughout nature on all planes of human thought. There is one less obstacle to viewing perfection in its true setting.

And that fact, among others, brings us now to consider again the proposition that man's effort can influence the course of human, as well as strictly physical, events in one direction, or the other.

5.

From personal observation and experience, we know that a human decision, for or against one course of action as compared with another, is capable of influencing, and does indeed influence, the direction in which a sequence of events moves. A choice may change the course of a person's education, or of an outing planned for the week-end, or of a nation's history.

Ideas, personalities and rules, authorities, responsibilities and cross currents, tangible and intangible circumstances, are among the various factors involved in a decision and its consequences. The fact that human choice can change, at all, the course of events raises questions as to the degree to which such influence can be exerted effectively and constructively or, in other words, as to what extent human decision can change the course of events within the bounds of natural law. And, in general, what are the powerful means of implementing human decision through personal effort?

To begin with, effort is not an ordinary exertion nor an aimless striving. Effort implies reaching voluntarily toward a definite objective. It is characterized by an urge from within that willingly chooses to put forces and energies to work toward the accomplishment of a specific aim.

Consider, first, and in brief, the importance of physical means. In the course of events, a system of physical force and energy, highly organized by man and brought to bear on moral issues, is a tremendously strong means of implementing human decision. In fact, there is only one systematic, temporal means mightier than the physical, namely, the effective moral order itself. Lacking such an order in being, the outlook is for those who worship physical force to gain, if not to keep, the upper hand. In itself, and as far as it goes, physical nature is the truth, but not the whole truth, only a part of the all-powerful truth.

Within a community, the system of physical force and energy needs to be integrated with the spiritual ideals of the supreme principle, in order to form the most effective instrument available to human effort from day to day. In keeping with our general theory of benevolent supremacy, this book is of the persuasion that the system of Christian morality—the real system thereof, not a counterfeit—is the most powerful design on earth. Therein, human decision can work with, instead of upon, the force of existence itself, conscientious effort becomes, or is capable of becoming, practically invincible.

According to our definition of thought, the original forces that manifest themselves in the working of human effort are the forces of ideas, or concepts. The idea is causative. The thought, in order to fulfill itself, must precede the deed. Freedom of choice, by its very nature, is intended to foreshadow the right decision. Saint Augustine could have been working on an idea of this kind when he said, in substance, and abstractly enough, "Believe truly in God, then do as you will."

The ideals accepted as true by a person's mind determine the character of his conscientious effort, if not of the consequences. The circumstances in which the effort is actually made are analogous to matter and energy which can be put to work for, or against.

Now, conscience can be defined easily, by rote. It is the mental faculty by which a choice is made between right and wrong. In the abstract, conscience is a term for moral consciousness. The faculty of choice is implicit. So are standards of perfection, be they true, or false, standards. And since, concretely, a contrast between ideal and actuality is always present, conscience and the emotions are inseparable friends, as well as relatives.

Instinct, as compared with conscience, has the more obvious pattern of the two, more obvious at least from the standpoint of the set patterns of form and behavior that are common to the species. Unfairly leaving other animate existence, such as our pine tree, to its own devices, one definition of instinct takes it to be "a natural, spontaneous impulse, or propensity, in the lower animals and in man, moving them without reasoning toward action essential to their existence, preservation and development."

In general, the indications are that, from generation to generation, instinct is a native or inherited faculty, not learned. It is highly complex, psycho-physically. It always involves an end, or goal. It is closely related to the welfare of the species and of the individual members of the species.

The present argument would have nothing to add to usually accepted definitions, such as the foregoing, were it not for our theory, and our findings so far, in regard to the nature of thought—that, first and last, all of existence is in terms of one great concept of reality, perfect in design and operation, in whole and in part.

The truth is waiting to be discovered or revealed to us in ever greater measure and degree, our argument holds. Suppose we add to this assumption a working hypothesis, to the effect that each spark of life which we call a human being has a faculty for keeping in communication with the source from which its being and its strengths originate, and for being governed by the laws that spring from the same source.

In these days of instantaneous communications around the globe, of the remote control of guided missiles and whatever else, it is indeed the unscientific person who would insist that all channels of communication and influence are obvious. It is the unimaginative, as well as unscientific person, who would refuse to consider seriously the continuing bond between the created and the Creator.

In man, the faculty above taken for granted develops gradually into an ability of the mind. It grows into a mental faculty known to us, under more than one name, as instinct and conscience—and intuition—depending on the different circumstances involved.

Each mind has an inborn capacity—a capacity that varies by species and by individual within a species—for working within, and as a part of, the whole scheme and pattern of existence. The human mind, among others, has such a capacity. The potential of good conscience is as native to the human being as instinct is.

And, while we are about it, intuition, under our present terms of reference, is the mental ability by which directly to discern and interpret flashes of reality, directly rather than through the ordinary processes of thinking, processes that usually involve reasoning and an arrival at opinion through actual trial and error. In some ways, intuition seems to resemble instinct more than it does conscience.

The sun is there. Its light shines into a laboratory through more than one window. The truth is there, the true design of perfection. The force of the truth can play upon more than one of the faculties of the instrument which we call the mind. The human being, as a spark of life, conforms more or less to the absolute criterion which partakes of both the spiritual and the physical.

The dividing line between instinct and conscience seems to be more arbitrary than substantial. Under perfect conditions, instinctive and conscientious decision would be, no doubt, as one. In everyday affairs, however, a distinction between the respective areas of instinct and conscience involves more than an abstract reconcilement of one and more than one, or of temporal and eternal centers of equilibrium. That there is an actual difference between instinct and conscience is evidenced, for example, by the conflicts between the two that are observable in and around us, unhappy conflicts when false ideals have been taken into the mind as true, conflicts charged sometimes with a fierce and consuming emotion. In which of the two areas is man more likely to be able to influence his own fate?

In a system of reward and punishment, the answer to the question can be seen to revolve around the matter of personal choice, the degree of freedom of choice in one area as compared with the other. There are instinctive acts, such as a behavior common to the species and a bodily conformity to a set design, instinctive acts regarding which the mortal has no apparent choice with respect to the motivating thought.

There are moral issues in which, barring undue restraint or coercion, a person can have almost a full measure of freedom to choose conscientiously.

It is, then, in the area of conscientious choice and effort, which means of moral choice and effort guided finally by the spiritual ideal, that man is likely to have the greater authority to influence his destiny, if not to alter the origin of his attributes nor to affect the general framework of his existence and its system. The ideal is an inevitable factor in the living of a human life. The character of the ideal is a factor of the utmost importance.

That is how our evidence regarding ergs and dynes and conscientious effort figures up. Our initial hypothesis remaining unchanged in regard to the supreme principle, the doubters of the 19th and 20th centuries, A.D., have yet to offer a better explanation of man and the universe than the Biblical concept of creation.

CHAPTER SEVEN

Religion and Politics

"He who shall introduce into public affairs the principles of primitive Christianity will change the face of the world."

BENJAMIN FRANKLIN

WE have defined politics in an earlier chapter. What, also, do we mean by "religion"? We hear people say these days that communism is, in fact, a religion. What is the distinguishing quality of a religion?

The word religion comes from a Latin root that has to do with "revering the gods." There is also a Greek connotation of "to heed," or "to have a care."

By formal definition, religion is the outward, or physical, act by which men indicate their inner, or spiritual, recognition of a god, or gods, having power over men's destiny and to whom obedience, service and honor are due. So the generally accepted definition of the word religion implies the existence of a superhuman and everlasting authority in the affairs of mankind. Unless a context indicates to the contrary, the term "religion" is taken, in the present volume, to include the eternal element of the spiritual. It is distinguished by the quality of a worshipful belief in the divine.

In a less pointed interpretation of the word, however, religion can signify a devotion, or fidelity, to any "principle or practice." This meaning is general enough to apply to widely different concepts. Politically, it could be made to apply to socialism and communism, or to other ideologies. It could apply to a special aim or concrete ideal, such as good physical health. Or, we can say, for instance, that it is wise to avoid, religiously, any ill-principled and chronic debt, either private or public.

Religion and politics! In our country—during the first half of the present century, at least—there has been noticeable a strong tendency in public policy and, presumably, a like trend in much personal thinking, to go to an extreme in trying to keep religion and politics in compartments completely separate from each other. Such has become largely the habitual, as well as familiar, attitude. In politics, we are supposed to think about ability to pay. In religion, we are supposed to think about ability to pray. Religion should be kept out of politics, and vice versa. And a good idea that is, too, in a number of ways.

But a general prohibition, or an accepted axiom, of this kind bears some analysis. Perhaps there has been a misunderstanding about what is essentially Caesar's.

Does the arbitrary prohibition refer to a separation of religion and politics in the abstract? Or does it refer to Church and State, and, if so, to what kind of separation—and to which Church and to which State? Does it mean separation in the sense of legal disestablishment of the Church as far as the application of public taxes to support Church expenses is concerned? Or does it mean that the guiding principle of the Church and the guiding principle of the State, the religious and the governmental principles, should be kept separate?

Fortunately, the citizens of our democratic republic are

in possession of political documents, among others, in which nearly all such questions are answered rightly, as well as explicitly, for anyone interested enough to investigate the subject for himself. Take, for instance, the Constitution. Freedom of worship is provided therein, freedom of religious worship. It is basic to the Constitution, that direct interference of the State in the religious affairs of the Church, and of the Church in the political affairs of the State, is not to be countenanced.

But what about the last of the several questions just asked above? What about the relationship between the guiding principle religiously and the guiding principle politically of, for example, the American people under the Constitution?

A perusal of the actual lines of the American Declaration of Independence and of the United States Constitution makes it clear that the Christian principle is recognized as the final strength politically, as well as religiously, upon which the American Republic was founded. And this truth has carried forward through the years.

To quote one of the greatest leaders in the history of our nation, President Lincoln—"Tear down the Christian flag and Old Glory will sink of her own weight."

In terms of the principle of our government, and of its system of checks and balances, the Church and the State each has its living rôle to play in the community, to fulfill, in keeping with ideals which are mutually strengthening. Concretely, it is impossible, without unfortunate consequences, to separate either the religious ideals or the political ideals of a nation from one and the same high source of power. Sooner or later, in the event of such separation, the system weakens because, within itself, it has become confused and divided, lacking a principle that is absolute.

The roles of the Christian churches and of the American

political parties are distinct and separate. In matters of practice and procedure, it is naturally a rule that unity, for unity's sake alone, is not a good enough purpose. But, at sovereign level, unifying principle, not a monopoly of ways and means, is involved.

The Constitution embodies unifying principle, under which religion and politics in the United States have one of the greatest opportunities willingly to sustain and strengthen each other that the world has ever seen. Under the liberty of our democratic republic, the opportunity amounts to a freedom to exercise mutual good will, voluntarily.

The community is made up of individual members, each of whom is of a dual nature, in that the human being is directly and, at the same time, indirectly responsible to the Supreme Being. He is responsible to his Creator, first, as an individual, and, second, as a member of human society.

And, if there be an equal opportunity for each human being to attain a perfect existence, it follows that, in common justice to mankind, there is essentially but one standard of perfection—one absolute standard manifested variously—by which to gauge all human thought and act in terms of what is best for the existence of the individual and of the community.

In a truly democratic republic, religion, through the will of the people, sets forth the eternal rules that are to be implemented by the temporal authorities of the State. Various fields of public interest are concerned. For example, there is the field of education, a subject to be considered further in a later chapter, particularly because of its immense influence on the sentiment of the sovereign will, which we call the will of the people.

Appropriate political measures tend to foster true religion. In turn, the force of religious thought, under "the Laws of

Nature and of Nature's God," can be brought to bear politically in the choice of right ideals and of moral aims, and
ways and means, through the representatives elected by the
fellow countrymen of, for example, this American Republic
of ours.

"Religion," Karl Marx had said, "is the opium of the people." In examining that statement, which stems logically from
the concept of atheism, there are a number of well-supported
facts which could be recorded. One fact is that politics is the
"religion" of the communist.

As an avowed atheist, Lenin evidenced the conviction that
true religious principle and Marxism can never be reconciled.
He proceeded, accordingly, to develop the theme of an
unconditional surrender of the individual to the central will
of the communist State. His theme is the contradiction,
rather than the Hegelian antithesis, of the religiously inspired
ideology of personal freedoms under democratic rule.

2.

The concept of a superhuman authority and power, with
a question mark about a corresponding responsibility, is older
than recorded history, if we may judge by the relics that
have come to light.

At first, man seems to have pictured divinity in the form
of many gods of various stature, rather than as one God
manifest in various forms. The Greek and Roman gods, and
the Norse, are examples of forcefully inspired and vigorously
inspiring thoughts of divine power. The Hinduism of our day
—lost, as this religion is, in mysticism and lacking, as it does,
the element of the absolute by which to find itself—has still
to progress beyond the polytheistic stage.

In the East, desires for, and love of, wisdom resulted in

elaborate structures of thought. Great philosophies developed, in answer to the questions of daily life. Two of the foremost, or the two foremost in point of widespread influence, are Buddhism and Confucianism.

The philosophies of Buddha and of Confucius are basically different in their respective attitudes toward life and, in addition, the outgrowths of each have become many and varied. There is no desire herein to lump the two together. Confucianism is hopeful in its system of moral precepts for the appropriate management of society. Buddhism, in spite of its lofty concepts, is essentially a doctrine of despair. But they have a special circumstance in common. For all of their respective and mighty ethical values, neither of these two philosophies was intended by its own author to be a religion. The theological elements later added to each do little but confuse the eternal issue.

It is more than surprising, it is cause for alarm, that presumably intelligent and well-informed, as well as powerfully situated, people in our day, can think seriously that all religions, and all philosophies with religious overtones of good intent, are really the same, basically, in their respective ideals and belief. Such a view is a big mistake that amounts to a dangerous trap of the highest order.

Philosophies and religions which do not distinguish between day and night are really, as well as figuratively, left groping around in semi-darkness. They fail to see, not only that evil finally destroys itself, but also that those who do not actually take sides against evil are much more than likely to be destroyed along with it. "He that is not with me is against me." Philosophies of the relative, including comparable schools of religious thought, are fundamentally different from religions which recognize an absolute distinction between good and its opposite, evil.

I am reminded of a strangely symbolic, little room, off a side corridor at ground-floor level in one of the "United Nations" buildings in New York's Manhattan, symbolic of how far these still truly United States of ours have allowed themselves to wander from the source of their early and later strength.

It is inclined to be a wedge-shaped room of modernistic angles, curtained walls and a funereal air, along with a dozen chairs, or so, lined up in three, or four rows. In some ways, it looks like a small after-thought but, in design, it is in keeping, nevertheless, with the adjacent territory, which includes a vast expanse of floor and balconies and height of ceiling, in the form of a main gallery and lobby of the building itself. Here the architecture features bare physical elements of strength, such as unsheathed beams and girders, and walls of glass. The wedge-shaped enclosure was still referred to, the last time I visited the building, as the "Meditation Room." In fact, there was a sign outside its door to that effect.

The "United Nations" is an organization to which the United States is committed by treaty agreement—and treaty law of the United States ranks with the Constitution itself— but the UN officially does not recognize the divine principle. So the Meditation Room seems to be by way of a compromise. It could be used to take the place, more or less, of a chapel for any authorized person in the outfit, or for any visitor who might be unorthodox or "reactionary" enough to want to meditate, for instance, about God and His laws.

Toward the front of the room, or pseudo-alcove in question, there is—or was—a potted plant, unflowered and unflourishing. It sits on a pedestal of medium height, presumably to center the attention of those who meditate. Not that this book has anything against potted plants, but the contrary! It is more carried away with them, however, when they stay in character without the mechanistic touch. It likes them, for instance, in the sun on the window sill of the back parlor.

It will be worthwhile, as well as practically unavoidable, to think more about the UN, from time to time, as we proceed. But there are the religions of absolute principle for us to think most about—now, as ever. Said Epictetus, the Stoic philosopher, in Rome's early days of empire, "Think of God more often than you breathe."

From among the many and conflicting thoughts about religion that appear to have accompanied and influenced man's emergence from savagery and barbarism, there finally are recognizable the concepts of one God and of moral law. And as far as we know, these are comparatively new ideas in the world, ideas that had not yet taken form in man's earlier history. In contrast to the duration of all the ages past, it has been only somewhat over three thousand years since Moses brought the Ten Commandments down from Mount Sinai to the people of Israël.

The world owes a never-ending debt of gratitude to the faithful of the Jewish religion. In spite of nearly all manner of trial and tribulation, once the Jews knew the truth of the revelation of one God, the personal faith among the people carried through to sow the seeds that showed forth, not only in Judaism, but also in many of the teachings of the Christ.

In the path of One God, Almighty and Most Merciful, there followed also the great Prophet of Islam, Mahomet.

It is not the mission of this volume to enter the arena of the unhappy conflicts among Christians and Jews and Muslims, the followers of the three great religions just mentioned. It is more a part of its mission to stress the bond and the potential forces which they have in common. While this book is explicitly of the Christian persuasion, and also ends in being unequivocally of the Christian faith, it would be ungrateful, indeed, not to pay its respects also to the good deeds of both the true Muslim and the righteous Jew, as well as to the magnificence of the religious principle by which each is inspired.

Throughout the world there also are many other designs of religious thought, from the ancient to the modern. There are many practices thereof, particularly as relates to the political, which it would be of value for us to consider in this chapter, if we could do so within present limitations.

It is especially a temptation to try to follow a thread of thought about the relationships of religion and politics through the Middle Ages, up to the beginning of the scientific era of the present. At least, we can be tempted now to make a few notes about the corresponding sequence of mediaeval events.

3.

The Middle Ages, so-called in the manner of speech of the Western world today, are the centuries that came between ancient and modern times in the history of Europe.

Arbitrarily, the mediaeval period is taken generally to include the different events and the various climates of thought that prevailed from the time of the fall of the Imperial city of Rome, and of the Roman Empire in the West, to the days of the renaissance of the Graeco-Roman, or classical, arts and letters in Western Europe. In other words, the Middle Ages lasted about a thousand years, or from around 400 A.D. to 1400.

The early centuries of the Middle Ages are also referred to as the Dark Ages. At times, the lamps of knowledge and of wisdom were barely kept alight, and then only by the unifying force of the Church of Rome, the Church of Christendom in the West. The Emperor Constantine, in 313, had made Christianity a legal religion by the Edict of Milan.

Feudalism is the name given to a political system which, during the Dark Ages, sprang from the grass roots of Gaul and neighboring regions of the former Western Empire. Lacking a civil authority capable of securing law and order throughout diverse and widespread areas, there grew up around local strongholds a relationship among persons of various stations and drawn together for mutual protection and other benefits.

The feudal design was, by nature, a pact in the face of a common threat. The parties to the pact were joined in a systematic undertaking that involved, among other terms, the tenure of land by the vassal, in fief from the liege lord under whose banner a vassal bore arms.

In spite of numerous shortcomings, it was a sturdy and chivalrous new beginning and, above all, the community was in possession of a spiritual principle of limitless strength for man's guidance. The explicit Christian principle had survived Ancient Rome. Feudal civilization was to begin again the long, and often ill-inclined, march toward an era of real enlightenment all around that, today, still remains to be achieved.

It is surprising how impatient many people are with the spiritual workings of the universe. The agnostics and the atheists are particularly so. They neglect the evidence that it took man hundreds of thousands of years to comprehend the deliberate and purposeful use of the simple physical principles that enabled the rise of neolithic culture. In comparison to such lengths of time, a thousand years or so, in learning to apply a new concept of spiritual law within the community, does not seem unreasonable.

Toward the end of the Dark Ages, Charlemagne and King

Alfred the Great were among the great temporal Christian rulers. And in 1095 there began the first Crusade.

There were nine Crusades in all, the last ending in 1272. The illustrious names of the Crusaders range all the way from Godfrey de Bouillon, Peter the Hermit, Richard the Lion Hearted, and Louis IX, Saint Louis of France, to the Emperor Frederick I of Germany and to Prince Edward, later King Edward I of England.

In time, however, these expeditions became fairly routine operations against the Muslim opponents, termed infidels, who continually threatened the eastern outposts of Christendom. From the viewpoint of centuries later, we can call attention also to the brilliant period of Muslim thought from, say, the 9th to the 11th century A.D., as evidenced in the great universities that flourished in Damascus and Bagdad, in Cordoba and Seville.

Largely beyond the orbit of Christendom, this was also the age of the exploits of Genghis Khan, the Mongol conqueror, whose forces, armed with psychological as well as physical weapons, swept westward from Asia to the gates of Vienna—and then vanished in the direction from which they had come, as swiftly as they had arrived. His grandson, Kubla Khan (1215-1294), ruler of China, is said to have asked the West for Christian enlightenment for himself and, possibly, for his vast empire. As an example of opportunity lost, the request, to all intents and purposes, was never met.

But, in regard again to the Crusades, it remains to give them more their due. Their impact upon Western thought, word and deed turned out to be immense.

The early Crusades brought the chivalry and the simple Christian faith of the feudal West into collision with, and later into association with, the effete and disillusioned Roman Empire of the East, an empire disillusioned politically and morally, if not entirely so, in regard to the Christian faith itself. The aim that had originally inspired the Crusades was to regain, from the Muslims, possession of the Holy Sepulcher of Our Lord. And, in fact, a Kingdom of Jerusalem was established accordingly, under the auspices of Christendom, and lasted almost two hundred years.

The actual operations of the crusading forces, militarily and otherwise, contain, however, not only wonderful examples of individual heroism and Christian devotion to a chosen cause, but also horrible examples of a lack of integration of aims and acts in terms of the Christian principle itself. Near and far, the struggles for power between religious and political rulers were increasingly the order of the day.

But hopeful news was also in the making. Good news is to be found, for example, in the development of a philosophy which, in keeping with an Aristotelian approach, reconciled reason and faith, and set about the overcoming of essentially divergent views that were then in progress in religious thought concerning the design of life. Or, to be more specific, a systematic exposition of theology in abstract terms of philosophical principle—an exposition known as Scholastic Philosophy—was developed powerfully, and set forth clearly, by the Italian churchman, Saint Thomas Aquinas, at the middle of the 13th century. This system is now the official philosophy of the Roman Catholic Church. And it is anathema to the communist and his fellow traveller.

One of the truly great books of all time, it may be added to our record here, was published on the same subject centuries later, in 1916. It is entitled "A Handbook of Modern Scholastic Philosophy," and is by the late Cardinal Mercier, of Belgium, with the collaboration of professors at the University of Louvain.

As consequences in large part of the Crusades, not only were there many changes in the points of view of the peoples of Europe, but also the ferment of iconoclastic ideas had begun. In the 14th and 15th centuries, the revival of classical knowledge stirred in the Italian peninsula, in cities such as Florence and Pisa—and, likewise, in the seafaring states of Venice and Genoa, the forerunners, if not the prototypes, of the great trading cities of the Hanseatic League in the North.

The name of Petrarch, as a man of letters, is associated especially with the first sign of the classical revival. From points of vantage in Italy and southern France, he was leader of the lighter vein of "humanist" thought in the Italian *risorgimento*. Morality is a mixture of the temporal and the eternal values, balanced in terms of the principle in common. The rebirth was a reaction against an underemphasis of the importance of the temporal in everyday affairs.

In the next century or two, the Renaissance was well advanced in France and Burgundy. It was under way also in other parts of Central Europe and in England. It was manifested in bitter religious conflicts and in mutual persecutions among people of differing religious opinion within western Christendom. It was marked, in addition, by the overthrow, through discoveries in the scientific field, of previously accepted ideas regarding various physical phenomena.

Further impetus to the rebirth of lay knowledge came from the migration of scholars westward at the fall of Constantinople to the Turks in 1453. America was discovered by Columbus in 1492. A few years later Vasco da Gama journeyed by sea from Portugal to India, around the Cape of Good Hope and along the African coasts.

Gunpowder had made its appearance in the West soon after the end of the Crusades. Printing by movable type came into use in Europe, in 1454, at Mainz, to be exact. And still our would-be thread of thought has failed to touch upon countless other events that also have led up to the present.

For the most part, the Middle Ages were a failure governmentally. The religion and the politics of Christendom emerged unreconciled from the turmoil of mediaeval times. But even a failure can serve as a good example of what not to do.

Temporal power naturally failed to *force* man to be truly religious. Temporal power is now trying, no less blindly, to *force* man to worship the State. In the absence of a clear recognition of the nature of human thought, and of the personal faculty of decision, there has been an awful similarity between the religious and the political persecutions man has endured as a result of mistaken ways and means by which to further the good intent.

Meanwhile, some people seem to derive much satisfaction from blaming the ills of the world on religious principle and, in particular, on the Christian principle. Christianity has failed, they say. Look at the awful record. The principle does not work.

Maybe. But it is respectfully submitted here that, if any man be so blind or unwilling as not to recognize the nature of the Christian principle and its system, or so lacking in imagination, industry and common sense as not to have learned how to make good use of its ideals and its laws through education and a benevolent authority, through good example and divine worship, it is because of no fault of the principle itself.

The Christian faith represents the greatest hope of the world—for one reason among others, because it envisions God as willingly responsible for His own creation. He has not only the authority, He has also the responsibility in the measure which His creation willingly obeys His laws. It is essential that this be a fact, if the eternal system of human existence is to make perfect sense. Otherwise, the prototype of existence fails to fulfill itself as an ideal for the guidance of men. Authority and responsibility go together. To hold authority without accepting a corresponding responsibility is tyranny.

If a man does not understand the law of gravitation, or does not recognize the physical principle involved in electronic devices, does he blame the law and the principle? Not often. He is more likely to bestir himself to find out what mistake he has been making in his effort and to try to rectify the error.

It is, likewise, not the design of human existence, nor the source thereof, that is to blame for the relative shortcomings and the apparently outright failures to be observed among mortals. Ignorance and lack of wisdom are at the root of mistakes. Misuse of the supreme and integrating principle tends only to obscure, not to alter, the laws of existence, its forces, its energies and its system, all of which naturally lend themselves to human progress toward perfection, not only in religion, but also in politics.

CHAPTER EIGHT

On Evolving Toward Perfection

OWEN WISTER, the late author of "The Virginian" and other novels of memorable appeal, has one of his characters remark, "We are no longer a small people living and dying for a great idea; we're a big people living and dying for money."

Well, it is to be hoped that this judgment of us can be considered as only fictitious. If it were, and still be, a really accurate description, if money for money's sake be really the American people's aim, may the oncoming generations be educated to look more beneath the surface. Somehow they will be.

Not that money is, in itself, evil. It is a purchasing power which is potentially either good or bad. Money represents an authority, and carries with it a responsibility, which can be turned to either right or wrong purpose in the instinctive, human urge toward perfection. Both the authority and the responsibility, rightly viewed, are to be desired.

In all animate existence, there is, in fact, an element and potential of growth, an urge toward perfection, which, as we have already noted, is lacking in the purely physical changes of the inanimate. Around the spark of life there is evident an animate economy that represents a practical system of adjustment of available means to the end, not only of continued being but also of an evolution toward ever better conditions of existence throughout the course of life.

The word evolution has a flavor of materialistic determinism that tends to neglect the element of animate instinct and of human effort. This flavor is to be guarded against. It leaves a bad taste. Evolution actually comprises not only a mechanistic "rolling out," but also a conscious direction—at least that is true in respect to man.

We think and comprehend as humans. We are interested primarily in human progress toward perfection. That fact leads us now also to narrow the field for present inquiry, by deciding what kind of perfection, among those discernible by humans, we intend mostly to consider in this chapter. Perfection is a word that brings to mind many kinds of excellence. It implies wholesomeness in all respects. To perfect is to complete, to finish or to carry to the end—a meaning which fits in with the concept of an actual fulfillment of an idea.

It is a word that brings to mind, for instance, various kinds of physical, moral or spiritual excellence, as the case may be. There is excellence at rest or in motion. There are standards of perfection with respect to design or as to systematic operation. There are ideals of personal perfection and as to what the circumstances of life within the community should be, ideals in terms of the temporal and also of the eternal. Finally, there is the absolute perfection of the Supreme Being, of His laws of nature and of His design for life, for human life among other kinds.

Each one of us, naturally, is seeking for a lively peace of mind. We do not work on earth for some sort of oblivion or some vague absorption into the infinite, or for some impersonal view of a cosmic religion reducible to a mathematical formula. We are really after a personal peace of mind alive forever with a health of body and of soul.

Human life on the Earth, in word and deed, is made up

of the fulfillment and the attempted fulfillment of ideas. Together, we are after the perfecting of a working system in everyday affairs. We are after a design for living, a design in common, that, under a continual supremacy of good will, is integrated, in principle, and in practice, with the various ideals that comprise all-around excellence in everyday affairs. It is excellence as a whole that approaches nearest the absolute.

Among the many aspects of perfection, we might choose now to inquire, for example, into the general working relationship that exists as among the respective forces of virtuous ideals, the forces that mark the well-inclined human effort. Is it ever possible in such a relationship for a virtue to become a vice? We might also think some more about good and evil personified, as related to a system of good will among men. And, then, there is, too, the matter of human evolution toward perfection, as related to that subject of common interest which we refer to as survival.

2.

Throughout the relatively brief record of the human race on this earthly sphere—the medium-sized sphere of the comparatively small solar system which, as far as we are concerned from day to day, is the physical center of the universe —there is noticeable an unevenness of progress in the fulfillment of one idea as compared with another. Similarly, progress in one field of human interest can outdistance advancement in another area.

A condition of general advancement seems to be a matter of the equilibrium among various forces of like and unlike character, and also a matter of trend in one direction, or the other. Human affairs are well-inclined, or the reverse, depending not only on the relative strengths of the opposing forces at work, but also on how the forces similar to each other in character are balanced among themselves.

In a generally ideal situation, in a perfectly balanced condition, all kinds of excellence would have equal force, one with the other, all true ideals collectively would be as one. The importance of one right ideal or of one true virtue, would not be emphasized to the neglect and detriment of another. The material and the immaterial elements at work would play their respectively well-tempered rôles to perfection.

Quality and quantity, in practice, would look for guidance to their counterparts in the abstract. Quality and quantity in each field of concern would match equally the perfection of development in every other field. Omniscience would be of equal perfection with the freedom of the human will, in the complete assurance that only in God Himself are the law and the person joined absolutely.

It would be a great day all around—and fanciers of one-horse shays might make a note at this point that the reason Mr. Holmes' contraption in "The Deacon's Masterpiece" turned out to be imperfectly balanced, after all, was that it was solely physical. No wonder it went to pieces. There is, nonetheless, a collective ideal of perfect equlibrium, given nonphysical as well as physical ingredients, one that serves the useful purpose of lighting the way toward excellence, in general, as we have already noted in other context.

The ideal of a right equilibrium, in practice, moreover, is a criterion by which to add force to one measure as compared with another, in order to achieve a better inclined, instead of a worse inclined, course of action.

The choice of one intermediate course as against another, of some ways and means as compared with others, should be responsive to the needs of a given situation as estimated in terms of the entirely well-balanced ideal. Once off course, however, more emphasis must be given temporarily to one immediate direction, or to another, in order to get back to a true course, or to approach a true course for the first time. This is an especially important fact in a world that is imperfect, a world like our own.

It is a fact that offers a sound basis for the procedure of establishing priorities among plans and efforts, and for trying different ways and means at different times and places. Perseverance is more than repetition.

It is a fact that shows up in all sorts of relationships that involve an equilibrium among abstract ideas as well as among deeds. To hark back to the wisdom of Aristotle for an example, what is just is not always equal. In a system of reward and punishment, such as the natural system of human life, an equal reward is not always just, some factors have to be weighed. Reward, in order to be just to all, needs to stay in balance with the specific accomplishment, not with the general idea of equality for equality's sake alone, a thought which we might flag also for further examination later on.

Many are the ideas containing various elements of virtue that, in terms of right and wrong, have gotten out of balance within themselves, or within their actual context of events— for example, during the lifetime of some of those among us who are still staggering around in the flesh.

Vague ideas of peace in the abstract, ideas that have led to wars. Ideas of personal charitableness that have become so confused as to be engulfed ever further in an ill-balanced State Socialism. A natural desire for a better existence that has developed into an almost general demand for an easy method of security, for a social security presumed to be safe in terms, mostly, of an unstable dollar.

Then, as another example, there is the matter of a whole-some respect for financial obligations of a duly established government, or sovereign power. This is a proper respect which has, nevertheless, gotten out of balance in the common effort toward the collective ideal. It is a respect which, in our country, has thoughtlessly allowed a dogmatic sanctity to spread around our ruinous public debt and to obscure the real nature of such a debt.

Public debts that unjustly mortgage the future—as, for instance, the chronic public debt of the United States, among others of the kind, now does—are wrong in principle. To prove the point, public debt is, by nature, self-liquidating. If it be not brought effectively into balance, as of the present time and place, by conscientious effort, then the debt tends to liquidate itself through currency inflation, or through default or repudiation, or through other means, including physical violence, if necessary, to restore a natural balance.

The existence of a collective ideal of well-balanced excellence shows up in situations around us every day or, rather, the need for such an ideal is evident. It is needed in conditions and events that range all the way from individual personalities and business enterprises to the affairs of State.

Within a national economy, progress within one field is related to progress in another in terms of the collective aim and of the common good. Even our old friends, the Dow-Jones averages, need a comparison between at least two categories of values in order to register and confirm a collective trend in one direction or the other.

It is in the domain of political affairs, domestic and foreign, however, that we can find, as of here and now, some particularly outstanding examples of disequilibrium. In the so-called Western world, one nation after another seems to choose its various policies largely without regard to, and apparently without knowledge of, an absolute criterion by which to weigh one aim and policy as against the alternatives.

It would appear that the science of government is in as confused a condition today, as were astronomy and chemistry and biology, for instance, at the beginning of the Renaissance some hundreds of years ago. And the precariously inclined balance in political affairs is no longer of only localized importance. For the first time, as far as we know, the unevenness in the general advance of knowledge as compared with wisdom becomes, at last, of critical importance to the whole world at once.

In defense of the excellent progress toward perfection in some fields of science, however, it is not true that a virtue ever becomes a vice. Some excellent developments do not keep abreast of others in the march forward, but the virtuous character of a good development is not changed thereby.

There is never too much of a good thing. The mistake, or the vice, is to be found in there being too little of other good things, as of the same time and place. Evolution toward perfection is a matter of well-balanced progress toward the collective, unified ideal.

3.

Since, in reality, there is an opposite to any particular ideal, and since the emotions are naturally stirred by the varying degree of difference between the ideal and the actuality, a clear mental image of evil, as well as of good, is a requirement for the proper functioning of a system of morality. For that matter, the same is true of any carefully organized system of human society, be its standard of perfection right, or wrong.

Any system involving a moment-to-moment equlibrium

between opposite ideas and their respective forces in motion can be thrown off balance and put out of order by a neglect of one element of the system as compared with another.

In the system of human society, for instance, a continual over-emphasis of the likelihood of reward or a neglect of the likelihood of punishment—or vice versa—tends toward disequilibrium and weakness in the functioning of the system as a whole.

It is true that, according to the Christian principle, the hope of reward is essentially more powerful than the fear of punishment, but that does not mean that the importance of the latter is to be neglected. The fact that too much effort seems sometimes to be expected of a human being with too little reward in sight, or any other disparity of the kind, does not alter the basic rôles of hope and fear, nor does it change the system of stewardship and of justice centered in an implied hereafter.

Anyhow, the foes of the system of good will, which is identified and advanced by true Christianity, have a familiar technique. These foes and their unwitting allies have a technique for confusing the thoughts of the well-intentioned member of a benevolently inclined community, or group, or nation, and thereby making the individual minds more open to destructive suggestion.

As Robert Burns has long since reminded us in the course of an especially well-seasoned epistle of advice—

> "An atheist's laugh's a poor exchange
> For Deity offended."

Part of the unfriendly technique is, however, to hold the concept of God up to smug ridicule, open abuse and all manner of blasphemy. In addition, it is to blur the image of evil. It is to distort the image of evil in such a manner as to lead to a lack of vigilance toward the mistakes and the punishments for which the evil image naturally stands.

Among human beings, there is a need for a personalized concept to stir the emotions to adore. Likewise, in a system of opposites there is need for a personalized concept to abhor. But it is difficult indeed to hate such a rakish and amusing, though fallen, character as Lucifer is usually pictured to be in our time and place. These days he seems to be pictured seldom as a person of cruelty and filth, or as a breeder of pestilence, suffering and destruction.

It is easier to hate someone who is less beguiling than the modern Lucifer. It seems easier to dislike some uncongenial neighbor who is only too visible, or to take exception to some "obviously" unworthy steward in life, than it is to imagine the embodiment of all evil, or to hate a vague or an heroic kind of Satan.

For many people, in fact, the former Archangel in question may have been, and may still be, relegated to the story books of long ago. The concept of the Evil One needs, nevertheless, to be revitalized in realistic terms and not lost. In the system of human existence, evil remains the opposite of good, no matter how the fact be pictured, for either religious or political purposes, or both.

Personally, the present writer finds it easier to dislike some people for no apparently good reason at all. If he never sees, nor hears again, of some—well, at least a few or more—of the people he has known, or read about, that will be too soon. From the standpoint of evolving, what is any one of us supposed to do, besides saying his prayers, about the existence of such a condition as that?

As usual, accepted ideals and set standards are involved,

no doubt. Perhaps it is a matter of expecting too much of other people, of expecting other people to be and to do more as we would like, which may, or may not, be what they should be or do.

From the start, one thing, among others, seems certain. Personal likes and dislikes are beyond coërcion, if not beyond subtle influence. Not only the imagination, but also the human will, is essentially free. The individual finally makes his own choice of an opinion concerning a person as well as of the standards by which to judge him. And the choice of the standards may well be the key.

On the moral plane, a general pattern of either friendliness or unfriendliness, of forgiveness or unforgiveness, of thankfulness or thanklessness, of either good will or ill will, is characteristic of any one of us. It would seem that in trying to evolve toward perfection, one of the main things for anyone to do about personal dislikes is to consider impersonally, at first, the elements and the workings of the system of good will itself.

It is impossible, and rightly so in an imperfect world, for any one of us to like every member of a community in equal degree. Nevertheless, a practical knowledge of the scheme and pattern in which human life exists can help nearly anyone to see, or to detect, the good in another person, whether the two be drawn together, or the reverse.

It is easier to view an uncongenial person with good will, if he be viewed in a general and habitual pattern of good will, than it is to consider him favorably as a person apart. Maybe it was the development of an habitual attitude of good will that, for example, enabled Will Rogers to say sincerely that he never met a man he did not like.

How to have a clear mental image of evil as well as of

good, how to give just due and, at the same time, to forgive the human being for his mistakes, how to "love thy neighbor as thyself"—these are subjects fundamental to a benevolent supremacy.

4.

In 1859, Charles Darwin, the English naturalist, presented his theory of evolution and, in the same year, his book entitled "The Origin of Species by Means of Natural Selection" also made its public appearance.

Charles Robert Darwin, to use his full name, was born in 1809 and died in 1882. As a young man he had voyaged around the world on an official British surveying expedition. In regard thereto he begins his Introduction to "The Origin of Species," as follows:

"When on board 'H.M.S. Beagle,' as naturalist, I was much struck with certain facts in the distribution of organic beings inhabiting South America, and in the geological relation of the present to the past inhabitants of that continent. These facts, as will be seen in later chapters of this volume, served to throw some light on the origin of the species—that mystery of mysteries as it has been called by one of our greatest philosophers. On my return home, it occurred to me, in 1837, that something might perhaps be made out of the question by patiently accumulating and reflecting on all sorts of facts which could possibly have any bearing on it."

Evolution, in the Darwinian sense, has come to be a concept to the effect that existing animals and plants have developed by a process of gradual, continuous change from previously existing forms. This theoretical concept, also referred to as descent with modification, comprises organic evolution as compared to inorganic evolution. The latter relates to the development of the physical universe from supposedly unorganized matter.

Now organic evolution does not oppose belief in the particular creation of each individual species, but it does oppose belief in the creation of each species as an immutable form within itself. In other words, it allows for changes within a given species. It does not, however, assert that one species develops into another species—an important point indeed. It implies only a common origin and substance of some kind, not an interchangeability of species.

Darwin had noted variations *within* a species, some of which variations were helpful to survival, and some of which were transmitted to offspring. Hence Herbert Spencer's phrase "the survival of the fittest." But Darwin did not find time to progress far enough with his great work, in order to be able, himself, to set forth a clear distinction between inheritable and non-inheritable characteristics.

Meanwhile, the Augustinian, Mendel—Gregor Johann Mendel, Austrian scientist and Roman Catholic priest—had been experimenting in his garden with the hybridization of garden peas. As a result, he discovered the laws of heredity which today bear his name, the Mendelian laws. In 1865, he announced his findings quietly, and without attracting much more than local attention.

It remained primarily for the Dutch botanist, Hugo de Vries, to re-discover the Mendelian laws of heredity. This de Vries did around 1901. That year he also announced his own theory of mutations, or suddenly-appearing, well-defined variations, as compared with the slight cumulative changes which had been noted by Darwin. But still all of this was *within* a given species.

Evolution is generally thought of as being a development from the lower or simpler form of animate being to the higher or more complex organism. But in this regard, there is also a note to be made concerning the growth processes of the ascidian.

The ascidians are species of tiny, aquatic organisms, belonging to the animal kingdom, and known as simple or compound tunicates, as the case may be. In contrast to the invertebrate structure of the adult, the larva of the ascidian shows many vertebrate characteristics, indicating descent from some vertebrate ancestor, and thus representing a retrograde evolution.

In other words, evolutionary development can proceed in either direction, even though usually from the lower to the higher form. And, in any event, it is good to have the assurance that a man cannot become exactly a sea-squirt, nor some other, unexpected animal.

It was Darwin's theory that seems directly to have touched off the furor over evolution as opposed to creation, although other scientific discovery of the age was taken to aid and abet materialistic aspects of the evidence. From within the controversy, however, or above and beyond the dispute, there emerges the fact that creation and evolution are not mutually exclusive at all. The two are not opposites, and the controversy in regard to their relative merits seems to be due to a big misunderstanding and mistake.

The mistake has to do with a choice of coördinates, or, say, with the chosen terms of reference. Waters can be still and deep, and, at the same time, many-colored. A table can be both square and massive. There are general qualities and forms respectively, within which special comparisons and analogies can be made.

There are different phases in the fulfillment of the cycle of a force and energy. So, also, it is in respect to the living of a life.

Creation and evolution are different phases of one and the same cycle, in which it could be that the finite and the infinite are also joined. As to the misunderstanding, the final choice is between creation and nothingness, not between creation and evolution. There had already to be something before it could evolve.

Both creation and evolution have their respective places and their special functions in the scheme of existence. The spark of life is clothed in various bodies, and follows different patterns, in response to the forces and the energies of its natural design. One of the designs is the human being under the superhuman law and order of the Creator and Preserver of all mankind—or so it can be reasoned with immense support from personal experience and observation, as well as from instinct and intuition and, normally, from conscience.

And, in regard to the present subject, there is at least one more point that now seems to be of special interest. It further concerns Darwin's term, "Natural Selection," which he centered in the physical domain. Until now there seems to have been a continuing dearth of comment to the effect that natural selection, or "the survival of the fittest," can be finally in terms of the spiritual principle rather than of the physical principle of existence, that survival can be within the coördinate system of the eternal principle instead of only the temporal principle.

Newton's law of gravitation is valid in special terms of reference. It is encompassed, not rejected, by the general law of Relativity. Similarly, the moral law of the Old Testament is valid in special terms of reference, and, in addition, is embodied as an integral part of the universal law of the New Testament.

Granted the seeds of true knowledge and wisdom, and a grain of real faith, there is a conclusion which is so indicated in our day as to be practically irrefutable. The conclusion is that evolution toward perfection, insofar as the human being is concerned, is in terms not only of the temporal, but also of the eternal.

The survival of the fittest is finally according to the absolute standard of perfection, which we know also as the principle of Christianity.

CHAPTER NINE

Law and Order

THERE is again the matter of the Sumerians, the people "of the rivers," who began to show signs of civilization some thousands of years ago along the banks of the lower Tigris and Euphrates.

From the beginning of time, as far as our own species is concerned, men have desired a reliable law and order of the land and have sensed the need for a dominant source of power above and beyond their everyday horizon. So it would seem, at least, from the record. The Sumerians were no exception to this rule, but they had a special approach to the subject as compared with a number of their contemporaries. The Egyptians, for example, had a habit of deifying their Kings and Pharaohs. Not so the Sumerians.

The Sumerians and their ideological descendants have conceived of the Almighty Power as superhuman but, at the same time, accessible and more or less susceptible to human supplication. Within the body politic, we are told, the Sumerians did not consider any one of the members to be perfect. Each person had to guard against a measure of imperfection which accompanied his worthiness.

Thus it was better for members of the community to take counsel in the face of mutual needs and individual interests. Intuitively, it was realized that, in community affairs, one human mind alone was seldom, if ever, enough of a judge and jury to insure, or reasonably to insure, all-around right answers. Joint consideration, rather than autocratic rule, could generally be expected to give more likelihood of a favorable and lasting recognition of the destiny of a people as a body.

This concept appears repeatedly throughout history. In the modern era, this American democratic republic of ours, is among the lineal descendants—if not always recognizably so—of the ancient Sumerian school of political thought, the school that believes in divine guidance in the affairs of State, as well as in the other affairs of the individual person.

The Age of Pericles, in Ancient Athens, offers the instance of an earlier vision than ours. It was a vision that embodied many, but not all, of the elements of the truth necessary for the mental image lastingly to fulfill itself, or to be fulfilled. But it is a classical example of high order. According to Thucydides, contemporary historian of the Peloponnesian War, we find Pericles saying in his great oration at the funeral of the first of the Athenian dead to be returned to their homeland from the conflict with Sparta:

"We differ from other States in regarding the man who holds aloof from public life not as 'quiet' but as useless; we decide or debate carefully and in person all matters of policy holding not that words and deeds go ill together but that acts are doomed to failure when undertaken undiscussed. For we are noted for being at once most adventurous in action and most reflective beforehand. Other men are bold in ignorance while reflection will stop their onset. But the bravest are surely those who have the clearest vision of what is before them, glory and danger alike, and yet notwithstanding go out to meet it."

2.

In physical nature and in the deeds of the world in which we live, order does not spring from disorder any more than disorder springs from order.

Thought is another thing again. There is a perfection of thought that is free from disorder. There is also the matter of human knowledge and wisdom with their mixtures of order and disorder. It is necessary, as usual, to distinguish between the absolute and the relative. And a concept of perfect order tends to fulfill itself concretely, not vice versa, or, at least, such is the case for the human being.

Actual order in an imperfect world, as compared with the order of the abstract design, or with the perfect circle of the master plan, is always relative in terms of the governing authority. From event to event, such order is a matter of equilibrium among moving forces under the law of a principle.

The equilibrium is variable from moment to moment, the natural law is constant, the true principle is changeless—these are always real terms of reference in a human community. The order therein is, furthermore, not only relatively right or wrong, but it is also dynamic as the result of the opposing forces of different thoughts, in particular, each thought bent on getting and keeping the upper hand of its opponent.

In some quarters, there may be another opinion in regard to the correctness of some of these statements. To be sure that we are considering the same subject as the persons who may disagree with the present views, it would be a good idea to know as clearly and as exactly as we can what is meant by order.

To identify this definition seems to be routine. Order is

a word that is used more than often. But the project, it turns out, could be somewhat of an education in itself. In a modern, international dictionary there are twenty-one, or more, meanings given for the word "order."

We find, for instance, that order can mean freedom from disturbance under the rule of duly enacted law or of other established governmental authority in a community. In that sense, we say that *order* is maintained in a community. Then there is also the meaning which has reference to a body of persons united by duties and rights in common, such as in the social *order*.

And there are the nine grades, or *orders*, of angels, which must have seemed more than quaint to many of the signers of the present Charter of the "United Nations," but not so to many of the signers of the American Declaration of Independence nor of the United States Constitution.

"For he shall give his angels charge over thee,
to keep thee in all thy ways.
"They shall bear thee up in their hands, lest
thou dash thy foot against a stone."

There is, however, another definition which better fits the word order as it is used in the caption of this chapter. This meaning concerns a regular or methodical disposition of the various elements that function in a system. It relates to an actual order of arrangement and, as an instance in particular, there is the policy of a government which, in accordance with the government's chosen ideals, gives precedence to various concrete aims and courses of action in an *order* of first things first.

For our present purposes, "law" is easier to define than order. A law is a rule or mode of conduct made obligatory, through some sanction, which is imposed by a controlling authority and enforced thereby in case of the violation of the law. Thus a law has fixity, and also has teeth. It is set for a purpose and is not intended to be treated lightly—and the usual definition takes for granted, without mention, the rewards and benefits that accrue to the law-abiding.

As pertaining to the present mission, there are two main bodies of law to be noted. First, there is the constant law of nature on the various planes of human thought, law which we have already considered, from time to time, herein, and are now on the point of looking into again from the viewpoint of the moral system of a community. Second, there is the man-made law into which we are scheduled to inquire specifically, from time to time, during the following chapters.

In advance of the latter, it is probably enough now to observe, regarding man-made law, that the closer human legislation and established mode or standard conform to natural law, the better for all concerned. The two bodies of law, above mentioned, are naturally intended to be connected in principle, and unless the human variety conforms accordingly it, the man-made law, can only cease sooner, or later, to exist.

On the moral plane, both the man-made law and the person of authority can vary as to degree of excellence. The evolution toward perfection in our own nation has resulted in there being a government of law rather than of person. More precisely, it is a government, not of individual person, but of law enacted by the will of the majority of the people. This procedure takes a leaf from the book of the ancient Sumerians, among others.

The principle of the United States Government is, under God, the will of the people. Thoughtlessly we may say merely the will of the people, forgetting, for example, some-

thing of vital importance in respect to the law and order of
the United States Constitution. The something is that without
true religious principle, such as originally inspired the Constitution, the spiritual element of morality, and consequently
morality itself, is abandoned, thus leaving brute force finally
to exert, for perhaps a long while, the ascendant power politically.

In regard to the moral organization of the community, it
is also in line with the working hypothesis of the present
argument that, under the laws of nature, there is, within creation, a systematic design of perfection for the moral order
of mankind. There is discernible in human nature, a regular
disposition of the spiritual and the physical elements that
function from event to event in a system of morality. It is
a disposition which we should view further in our chapter
on responsive government.

This book takes the position, as heretofore observed, that
the natural designs of the moral rule and of the moral order
are joined to perfection in the ideal scheme and pattern of
the system of Christian morality. For us mortals, so-called,
the supreme principle exerts its force through the ideal. The
spiritual ingredients of the moral rule are in the form of
abstract ideals which, in themselves, are changeless, whether,
or not, they have become personified, or otherwise sym-
bolized.

But, at a given place and time, what if, in actual practice,
a choice has to be made between two ideals, both of which
are essentially good, or among several ideals all of equal
quality? The question of precedence is one that we need to
consider explicitly within the general framework of any system of morality that is to be really workable, such as the
system of Christian morality is.

And again, within our present limitations, we shall have

to choose for special inquiry and examination only a few of the questions and the facts that concern the particular subject at hand.

We have already explored a little the subject of the source of human strength and being. The absolute importance of a worshipful belief in a God, Transcendent and yet Immanent; the power that comes of prayer; the good will among men in which godly love fulfills itself on earth—these facts are indispensable parts of Christian morality at work. They are facts which we have already tried earnestly to view in their real context.

That human life is a stewardship, under God; that the Atonement is the final hope of even the worthy steward in his strivings toward perfection; that thought is not created by the mind of man, but is primarily revealed thereto and partly discovered thereby—these are concepts which are already basic to the trend of the present argument.

In addition to the above matter of moral precedence, however, there are two questions which seem to be especially indicated for us now, as related to the systematic order of a benevolent sovereignty. We can consider them respectively in sections 4 and 5 of this chapter—with another look, beforehand, at the general idea of precedence.

The first of the questions has to do with one and more than one, as related mathematically and otherwise, under the law in common. It involves, mainly in the abstract, the importance of the whole, as compared with the parts, of a given system.

The second question is more personal. In fact, it is a question regarding moral law and order that ranks with those of the highest importance. How it be answered, particularly in the United States these days, promises to affect the destiny of all the people in the world. It would be indeed a triumph for communist aims of world domination if the West were to become convinced that it is wrong to use force, including physical force and energy, even in the good cause. What of the Christian precept "that ye resist not evil"?

3.

I have heard it said that there is an intelligent exception to every rule. It is a statement that takes in a lot of territory.

Without exception, human accomplishments in the world are governed by natural law right through to, and including, the final reckoning. Our findings allow, accordingly, for no exception to the love of God. The first and great Commandment is absolute. On the moral plane of abstract ideal and concrete circumstance, however, the idea of exception needs to be examined further. With reference to the question raised in a preceding paragraph, suppose there are two, or more, ideals, equally excellent in quality, which have been translated into corresponding moral rules.

Sometimes it is necessary, as of a given situation or event, to choose to follow one rule instead of another. It is sometimes necessary to do so for the purpose of preserving, say, a man-made law and order which has proved itself to be a worthy counterpart of God's design. In a righteous cause, for example, it is necessary to hold the upper hand, even though it may sometimes require what seems to be an excep-, tion to one as compared with another of the Ten Commandments. One way of defending such a course of action is to assume, on the evidence, that there is a moral exception to every rule but to the absolute law of a worshipful belief in the Supreme Being.

On the other hand, although the meaning in general may be clear, such phrasing still lacks exactness in respect to "exception." The matter is one not of an exception to any of the ideals and rules of good principle. Rather, it is a matter of precedence, or priority, among various courses of action aimed and guided in the light of the collective, or complete, ideal.

Both the individual, and the community as a social and political entity, need to recognize that the existence of priorities within the conduct of daily affairs is an unavoidable fact. The choice of one alternative or another is made inevitably, by default, if not affirmatively. And the fact of priorities, a fact which practically has the force of natural law, needs also to be identified by name. Rather than call it the rule of the intelligent exception, however, it would be more exact to call it *the moral rule of first things first.*

This is a rule in which there is a current precedence among alternative decisions. The choices are at various levels of authority and responsibility, as well as in terms of the general or the particular subject.

Of foremost priority, it would seem, there is the protection of the very existence of the godly community and its individual members. Protection is needed against those who threaten benevolence and, accordingly, threaten human life, temporal, or eternal, or both. It is a protection that shuns the defensive as soon as possible and chooses to advance against the threat. For the dynamic and integrating principle of human existence, itself, is the final standard, as well as the design, of perfection.

Likewise, among the ways and means that need continually to be fostered, one and all, there are priorities within such important areas as those of education and of service, public and private.

There is a footnote to be emphasized, too—most priorities are not to be permanently set. Balance and inclination being of the essence, as they are, to human progress in the midst of ever changing circumstance, the order of precedence also has, usually, to be open to change. It has to be open to continual review and, not infrequently, to temporary alteration, as may be found best, for the purpose of overcoming opposition.

Now a rule of precedence and timing, such as this, could become a travesty of natural law, were it not subject to the justice and the mercy envisioned by the two Great Commandments. Subject thereto, however, the moral rule of first things first is a requirement in a number of ways. For example, it has to be complied with, as our everyday surroundings show, in order for there to be operated conscientiously and with increasing effectiveness, a local police force or the armed forces of a nation, a local or a state-wide system of schools, a private enterprise or the United States Government, or any such man-made instrument capable of supporting a supremacy of good will within the body politic.

4.

Throughout many a generation, the fact of number and the uses of numbering have helped, and also intrigued, men in their progress toward knowledge and wisdom. One and more than one. Numerical relationship, in actuality and in abstraction.

The existence of only one of anything on the moral plane of human decision is, indeed, a generalization of such high degree as to border on the nonphysical altogether. There need to be at least two if there is to be an area of choice.

Consider one point of space, for example, or one instant of time. In everyday affairs, one point of space and one instant of time, respectively, are abstractions. Fused in the event, as of here and now, they together are a part also of the space-time continuum which seems to be a reflection of an eternal system of reality.

It would follow, by the way—follow logically, at least —that the imperfect events of the temporal world are abstractions from the viewpoint of eternal perfection. But there is actually no such dividing line in thought. All of creation is finally one system. Abstract and concrete are only relative terms. The two are distinctly different, but also parts of the same system.

In any case, for purposes of both abstract and concrete comparison, the mind of man needs more than one of anything *plus* one criterion.

The Graeco-Roman biographer, Diogenes Laertius, tells us much—or told us much, around A.D. 200—about Pittacus, one of the Seven Wise Men of Ancient Greece. According to his biographer, "Pittacus said that half was more than the whole."

On top of that, Hesiod, the Greek poet who flourished in the 8th century B.C., as did also Pittacus, says in his "Works and Days," and we quote: "Fools! They know not how much half exceeds the whole." Neither does the present writer. He would have to guess.

He could guess that it is an ancient plug for simplicity of organization and operation within an economy, or perhaps it is just a good word for clarity, brevity and exactness—or it may refer to some geometric twist of numbers well known already to most people.

Mathematics, according to scientific definition, is the study of numerical quantities and of the relationships between them, of spatial quantities and their relationships, and of various abstractions of these relationships.

Arithmetic deals with numerical quantities, geometry with spatial quantities. Algebra is an abstraction of arithmetic. In analytic geometry, algebra is used as an instrument to develop geometrical theorems by means of the introduction of a coördinate system. The analytical method is indispensable to a grasp of calculus, and so on.

Thus, we progress to the application of mathematics to modern physics. We advance to the techniques of applied mathematics with respect also to chemistry, biology and statistics, as likewise to a theory of mathematical probabilities. The latter is not to be confused, let us note, with the revelation of a moral trend that has been known to amount to prophesy.

So things ordinarily get along nicely in mathematics, abstractly at least. On paper, it is possible to work out a whole system perfect in order and arrangement—when along comes someone extraordinary, like the Francis Bacon of Elizabethan and early Jacobean times. The fact, he says, that the parts of a given system agree with one another is not proof of the system as a whole. Not that this was an entirely unknown fact. It was more a case of rediscovery.

It was a fact allowed for by Aristotle, for example, when he systematized his logic by the use of what he called categories. His categories, or ultimate concepts, were ten in number, we might add parenthetically. Namely, they were substance, quantity, quality, relation, place, time, posture, possession, action and passion.

It was a fact recognized by Saint Thomas Aquinas in his reconciling of reason and faith in terms of truth, a fact that shows forth in his *Summa Theologica*.

It is, at last, the same story in every field. Functionally, the whole is more than the sum of the parts but, at the same time, the whole is dependent on the parts jointly and severally. There is need for a supremely integrating principle.

The individual person is the unit of humanity but, at the same time, human existence—as an aggregate of persons, not as a number of lifeless parts—is, in some ways, more than any one person. Thus, even mathematically, it is possible to argue for either individualism or for the common weal.

As far as human life is concerned the argument could go on almost forever, if there were no criterion of absolute perfection.

5.

"Ye have heard that it hath been said, An eye for an eye, and a tooth for a tooth:

"But I say unto you, That ye resist not evil: but whosoever shall smite thee on thy right cheek, turn to him the other also.

"And if any man will sue thee at the law, and take away thy coat, let him have thy cloke also.

"And whosoever shall compel thee to go a mile, go with him twain.

"Give to him that asketh thee, and from him that would borrow of thee turn not thou away.

"Ye have heard that it hath been said, Thou shalt love thy neighbour, and hate thine enemy.

"But I say unto you, Love your enemies, bless them that curse you, do good to them that hate you, and pray for them which despitefully use you, and persecute you;

"That ye may be the children of your Father which is in heaven: for he maketh his sun to rise on the evil and on the good, and sendeth rain on the just and on the unjust.

"For if ye love them which love you, what reward have ye? do not even the publicans the same?

"And if ye salute your brethren only, what do ye more than others? do not even the publicans so?

"Be ye therefore perfect, even as your Father which is in heaven is perfect."

In these verses from the 5th chapter of the Gospel according to St. Matthew, there are to be found a number of precepts and admonitions from the Sermon on the Mount. Some are general in character, some more specific. All have a common element of absolute good will.

One of the most controversial of all of the precepts and, at the same time, one of the most important from the sovereign standpoint of good government among men, has been the statement "But I say unto you that ye resist not evil." Together with the illustrations which accompany it, this admonition seems to be a negation, not only of the concept of joining forces in the good cause, but also of the whole system of opposing forces which characterizes the moral plane of human effort. Or so it seems to be, in terms of the human being who is striving for, but has not achieved, a self-sustaining degree of perfection.

Is the precept in question a star to guide by, as are the Beatitudes which precede it in the Sermon on the Mount? Or, is it a concrete standard of perfection in the form of a rule of action on the moral plane?

Is this admonition, within itself alone, so completely self-sustaining as to be absolute in conscientious effort on the earth? Or is it a precept that is subject to varying priorities within the sequence of events? We really need to know.

In regard to the above questions there is an apparent difference between Biblical word and deed for us to ponder. Did Jesus resist the evil forces that were making "a den of thieves" of the Temple in Jerusalem? He did. And he resisted positively, not on the defensive. He seized the initiative, physically as well as spiritually, and cast out the offenders, even overthrowing their tables and their seats.

It would seem to be in the area of the apparent difference between the precept and the act that we can find the right explanation. And, in addition, is there not a parallel to be drawn and kept in mind, between the desecrators of the Temple in Jerusalem and the evils which the communists practice daily with regard to the religious temple and to the human temples of the soul which have come under the political control of the Kremlin and its allies? The facts answer yes.

The conflict between good and evil is not caused to disappear by ignoring it. It is inherent in the difference between perfection and imperfection. Good does not automatically overcome evil in the world of everyday affairs. Edmund Burke, among others, has put this thought, or some of its aspects, into words—"The only thing necessary for the triumph of evil is that good men do nothing."

Regarding the above-mentioned area of apparent difference between precept and act, Jesus, as the Great Teacher, spoke mainly in terms of the ideal and of the absolute standard of perfection. But He taught by His deeds and by the force of His example in addition to His precepts. As the Great Doctor, He gave special prescriptions to fit the particular case, as well as general prescriptions to fit all cases. His teachings are always within a context, and it seems that they should be considered in context accordingly.

The evidence with respect to His precept regarding resistance to evil is that Jesus was pointing out some of the many ways in which God, in all His goodness, is completely powerful. But man is not God. Man is not perfect enough to overcome evil automatically. Prayerfully, man has to strive to overcome evil by the various means available on the moral plane of everyday.

Any one precept is only a part of the whole design of absolute excellence. The ideal of the Supreme law and order is set forth in the last of the above quoted verses of the Scriptures—

"Be ye therefore perfect even as your Father which is in heaven is perfect."

—— *Part III* ——

Politics and Peace

CHAPTER TEN

Government Responsive to
Benevolent Ideal

"There are a thousand hacking at the branches of evil to one who is attacking at the root."

HENRY DAVID THOREAU

LIKE other physical laws of nature, the law of gravitation is entirely impartial—not because it is impersonal, but because, in itself, it is equally trustworthy for each and all persons. And a good thing it is, too. Where would we be now, I ask you, but for the dependable force of gravity!

Certainly not sitting around peacefully for a few minutes after lunch and looking out from one of the tall buildings at the tip of Manhattan Island to let our thoughts wander over the harbor where Hudson, and probably Verrazano and Cabot, came exploring at different times a few centuries ago.

For everyone, the salty boundaries of New York's Manhattan include the East River and the Hudson. Physically, if not otherwise, the island is impartial toward "every thing that is going on in the ordinary course of the business of life."

The East River is mostly a temperamental waterway from and to Long Island Sound. It is really no river at all, but it gives such a good and useful imitation of a river that it is better to let the idea rest. The Hudson, on the contrary, is a true river indeed. It is also known as the North River, for an old and good reason that comes from far upstream.

These two rivers, equally oblivious of the conflict and of the coöperation that can result from human effort, are busily engaged in winding "safe to sea," which sounds better, if less down to earth, than saying that they wind their way mechanically to the common level of an ocean. It is human nature, however, to personify anything that moves or that has a discernible being. Every river and any city, each neighborhood and every country, has its own personality. Thus, man gives expression, subjectively, to his intuition that there is a living and personal force beyond the mechanics of materialistic determinism.

For the human mind to be satisfied thoroughly that all goes well, the personal perfection of the Creator needs to be recognized as well as reflected in each element of His creation. The "Laws of Nature" are not without their powerful counterparts among the gods and goddesses of the Greeks, the Romans and the Norse. As compared with the mental picture of the living ideal, the graven image of a hero, or the lifeless body of an erstwhile leader, is not perfect enough to be a continual inspiration to human greatness.

So, when you come to think of it, there is really much more to the rivers bounding Manhattan than the two quantities of water that unite just south of the Battery. There is also the spirit of near and faraway places and of old and new endeavors, now transformed into the quality of the Upper Bay of New York harbor.

It seems to have no direct relationship to government policy, but it is a fact, and so not to be disregarded thoughtlessly, that you will find the Lower Bay after you pass seaward through "the Narrows" between Brooklyn and Staten Island

—not that we have time to go farther in that direction at present. After all, we are only out for a little change of scene before returning to the last part of our inquiry into benevolent sovereignty, the part that is supposed to look particularly into the matter of good will organized and operating politically.

On the way back up the harbor from the Narrows to the canyons and the myriad-windowed pinnacles of the massif that is today's Lower Manhattan—up the harbor channel that can still recall the din of welcome to homecoming U. S. Navy transports, like the famed "U.S.S. Leviathan," troop-laden upon the Armistice of World War I—you may notice how vulnerable the city is in an atomic age. Or, you can imagine some of the things that Henry Van Dyke is likely to have thought about when he wrote "America for Me!":

> "Where the air is full of sunlight and
> the flag is full of stars."

The southernmost square miles of Manhattan Island, from City Hall and Brooklyn Bridge down to the water's edge at the Battery, are the setting for the financial and shipping interests of an extraordinary port area. The area comprises now, not only the Statue of Liberty, but also over half of all the dock facilities in the United States.

In this center of many people's week days and of landmarks old and modern, there are buildings of the banks and offices of the brokers and the underwriters. There are the law firms and the headquarters of more than a few industrial corporations. There are the other variously related private and public enterprises which, either in a dignified or an undignified manner, depending on the circumstances, are lumped together and personified as "Wall Street."

Here are the floors of the Exchanges, where stocks and bonds, commodities and facilities, are bought, sold, or otherwise traded—in an atmosphere that avowedly is opposed to over-regulation, but that actually is not entirely free from a willingly accepted philosophy of enforced scarcity. For instance, there is the scarcity in regard to work days.

The old-fashioned provision of one of the Ten Commandments about working six days a week—not five, not seven, but six days a week—is out officially in Wall Street as well as in Washington, D. C. It remains to be seen whether or not this is a good omen—a good omen, that is, for the potentially, and currently, high mission of "Wall Street" and, likewise, for the morale of "the Government."

In regard to the latter, by the way, Napoleon is said to have estimated the importance of the morale factor, as compared with other factors in an actual situation, to be in a ratio of four to one.

The sights and the activity of downtown Manhattan are sources of never failing interest to me. But you might prefer to explore elsewhere. It is nearly always a mistake to take for granted that other peoples' preferences, especially in regard to a casual excursion, are the same as one's own.

Probably it is like the young man pointed out, opening oysters the while, back of one of the seafood counters over at the Washington Market near the Hudson River:

"How is the hunting this fall, Eddie?" a customer asked, in the course of reminiscing.

The young man back of the counter smiled, and nodded a little, as if he knew. "It depends on what you are hunting for," he said.

The less important the subject, the greater the variety of alternatives open to individual preference. The more important the subject, the narrower the field. But the less attention to unifying principle, the more important the incidental subject can seem to be. Well, maybe.

In spite of the new surfacing on the outside of its building, the Washington Market has been for more than a hundred years in the block of downtown New York which it now occupies. It does not have the Hollywood touch of the Farmer's Market in Los Angeles. It lacks the country air of the market in Bethesda, Maryland. I think that, in the earliest morning hours, better onion soup is likely to be had *Au Père Tranquille*, in Paris. I do not know the secret of the Washington Market's success so far.

Perhaps there is no secret about it. It is a matter of free enterprise among competitors who are organized under one roof, but each on his own standing, to offer a variety of good foods at reasonable prices—from domestic butter and eggs to wild game, by air, from Australia, Norway, Africa or elsewhere—under the safeguards of the United States Constitution, no less.

Many noon-hour finds have been made by downtown explorers. There was, until recently, the plaque which, for years, was attached to the side wall of the building near the entrance to the Police Station at 156 Greenwich Street. It read like a prelude to adventure:

> Division of Licenses
> Public Hacks
> Hack Drivers
> Dance Halls
> Cabaret Licenses
> Pistol, Tear Gas, and
> Religious Meeting Permits

The present ramble also gives an opportunity to say a few

words on behalf of, or in memory of, the Third Avenue Elevated Railway.

The late lamented "El"—it was the last of its kind in the Borough of Manhattan and, thus, of a scarcity value practically unequalled in recent railroad history—had not only a loyal personnel until the very end. It had also an appreciative, though dwindling, carriage trade from nearly all the walks of city life. Its trains rattled along deliberately in the open air at a well-nigh perfect rate of speed and they never ran off the track—almost never.

But its remaining days were numbered years ago and it was partly the El's own fault. It had not adjusted itself to the proper requirements of its changing environment, let alone being able to overcome the improper restrictions which it had to face.

"Simply by being compelled to keep constantly on his guard," Nietzsche tells us in *Ecce Homo*, "a man may grow so weak as to be unable any longer to defend himself."

Softened up in advance by the carefully chosen phrases of its adversaries, weakened by its exclusion from natural trade areas—its remaining terminus downtown was finally no farther south than Chatham Square—the El was chipped away. Its superstructure has been a victim of the torch, its supporting pillars have been pulled up, one by one, and wheeled out of sight.

The destructive tactics of the enemies of the Third Avenue Elevated resembled the ways of the Fabian socialists in their attacks on the capitalist system. The Fabian brand of socialism originated in England, you recall, and is named after some old Roman general because of his policy for the defeat of the Carthaginian, Hannibal. The idea was to wear Hannibal out, little by little. It is in a like sense that today's socialist is "progressive."

The course of action is also analogous, in a way, to the workings of the reliable physical principle of the wedge. The well-chosen wedge, under the impact of repeated blows, relatively weak though each blow may seem to be, tends finally to rend the strongest rock asunder.

A discovery of another kind and of different quality is one of the small windows high on the north side of Trinity Church, a window that pictures an ancient symbol, the Shield of the Holy Trinity. In the stained-glass of the window, the symbol is arranged as an ornate, equilateral triangle, the corners of which are joined by straight lines to the central point of the area enclosed by the three sides. The device has been adapted also to decorate more than one religious banner and students of the subject doubtless could associate it with the escutcheon of many a Crusader. Even in the prosaic walks of life the structural design, unadorned, seems to suggest the coördination of good aims, ways and means that look to one and the same source of strength.

It is a symbol to keep in mind long after this midday outing of the memory and the imagination has ended.

2.

If the genesis of the present volume had to be recorded, it would more than likely be listed under "conflict." It would probably be found in the conflicts of opinion and in the conflicting steps actually taken concerning government aims and policies, which your present recorder either encountered, or observed, during an endeavor of his some years ago in the Department of State.

In the trend of political affairs during the preceding decades, there had been a widening difference between his accepted ideal and the actual event. Questions raised by this difference had probably been building up a potential of personal concern for quite a while in advance of the endeavor just mentioned. Anyone can hardly spend a fair share of the workdays of his life in foreign banking, and in market places for exchange and securities at home and abroad, without beginning to wonder what in the world really goes on. But it was the impact of the unexpected proportions of the divergence of opinion at government-policy level, seen nearer at hand, that put in motion this search for answers.

After V-J Day, Major General John H. Hilldring, under whose command I had been on duty in the War Department during the then recent years of World War II, had retired from the Army and had become Assistant Secretary of State for Occupied Areas. Upon return to civilian status at about the same time, I again became a member of his office staff in Washington. It was more than a change from the Pentagon.

Under international law, the Hague Conventions and the decisions of the Supreme Court of the United States, the military commander, in areas occupied by the forces under his command, has all the powers of a *de facto* government. Depending on the circumstances, however, the commander may, or may not, actually be an independent authority. In the case of United States Forces, the commander looks to the United States Government for policy guidance as well as for military support.

It is a fundamental principle of international law that an occupying authority has, in addition to its rights, certain obligations to the inhabitants of the territory under its control. It must take whatever steps are necessary to secure public order. The latter cannot be maintained unless the continued operation of local trade and commerce is protected.

There are all sorts of ramifications. For instance, in the

financial field there is the monetary need, among others. There is the need and the obligation to establish an adequate and effective circulating medium, or currency.

The Office of Occupied Areas was an agency newly formed within the State Department for a temporary purpose. It was established to meet the special post-World War II need for the prompt formulation, coördination and transmission of United States policy, through appropriate channels, to the respective commanders of U.S. Forces engaged in occupation or military government duties, or both. The specific areas in question, occupied or liberated, as the case might be, were Germany, Austria, Japan and Korea.

There were few, if any, more active, post-war areas of interest from the standpoint of United States policy, nor areas in which the respective policies of world powers came more headlong into conflict, or, sometimes, into agreement. The resulting opportunity for close observation is the point now to be made rather than one dealing with personalities. High quality and discernment in the leadership of an Office of the State Department—or good and vigorous leadership in any Department or sub-division thereof—seemed to be unavailing at the moment in regard to the trend of the operation as a whole. The baffling inclination of United States policy toward self-defeat had been allowed to get out of hand, insofar as a prompt and final remedy was concerned. It was an untoward condition that stemmed from the root, not from the branches.

The essential weakness of the situation, policy-wise, was indicated in one way, among others, by an extreme of separatism between political and religious principle, a subject to which we have given some thought in a previous chapter of our inquiry. The clear indication of the need for a completely integrating principle was there for any and all, who would, to see—and, certainly, there was at least one person present who was slow to see it.

Concerning effective measures to correct an existing condition of the kind, it is not enough governmentally, in the face of evil, for the will of the people to be instinctively good. Even for the popular will to be imbued conscientiously with indistinctly related ideals, each of excellent quality, is alone not enough to insure success. The will needs to find and to develop mutually strengthening ways and means in every field, by which to express its character effectively.

Good will is not automatically good government. "Perfection is not an accident."

3.

Be the given problem primarily domestic or foreign, financial or political, or even superhuman, it is a safe rule that, at any level of authority and responsibility, policy is what to do and procedure is how to do it.

In policy formulation and implementation there are such elements as these—principle, standard of perfection, objective, course of action, and ways and means. Or, if you prefer to choose other words of like meaning, the classification can include, for example, the abstract, or the general, ideal, along with the concrete aim, the policy and the procedure.

For the analysis of a particular problem, according to one method at least, there are the facts bearing on the problem and, secondly, the other factors that enter into the discussion by way of arriving at a conclusion and a recommendation. It can all become pretty technical and, at times, perhaps too technical, if not too methodical.

The proposition is submitted herewith that, generally, the

best starting point for actually considering a problem, a governmental problem, for instance, is first of all to have as clear and exact idea as possible of what the ideal state and trend of affairs would be, the truly principled ideal and trend in respect to the point at issue.

What would be the particular ideal and corresponding aim, in a context of the whole scheme and pattern? What would be the standard of perfection, or the yardstick, concerning ways and means as parts of an integrated design? When right ideal and standard have been duly decided upon—and not before then—it is possible to proceed with a really comprehensive and orderly view of the various objectives, policies and procedures which are also involved in the problem.

Earlier in this chapter we noticed two apparently related phenomena. One was that the less attention there be given to unifying principle, the more important many kinds of incidental subject can seem to be. The other was that the more important the subject is, or seems to be, the narrower the field of choice. The two add up to a nice basis for wrangling.

From the standpoint of politics, we can go further and note a rule supported by actual examples in contemporary events. It is the general rule that, when a body politic, such as a nation, has lost sight of the meaning of the supreme principle of its being, the community tends to split, given time, into numerous political factions, with plenty of ill will as an accompaniment.

Conversely, a spectacle of such extreme individualism and political demoralization is a sure sign that a highly integrating principle of one kind, or the other, is lacking in the exercise of the sovereign power of the nation. In a truly representative form of government, such a condition of affairs brings under question the recognition by the people, themselves, of the nature of their supposedly guiding principle.

Our findings so far also bring us to at least one explicit conclusion in regard to political parties. It is that, in a country with a strong sense of right and wrong as measured by clear-cut principle and ideal, a two-party system is generally characteristic as well as desirable. This fact is in keeping with the truth that, in a system of opposites, supreme principle narrows the choice to two sides on fundamental issues and puts comparatively trivial matters in right perspective.

What does it mean for the future when the two parties come to resemble each other so closely that they can hardly be told apart? That depends largely on the nature of the resemblance. But, if the resemblance be in terms of a confusion in common, then, in principle and in practice, opposition arises from outside or there is a realignment from within the parties.

History also gives an answer to habitual political confusion and consequent disorder. It is that, given time, a strong and dictatorial hand is sure to emerge in some form, from some direction, to restore a unifying law—good, or evil, as the hand may seem, at first, to be.

Now statements, such as the foregoing, can be defended with facts and well-reasoned arguments, but it is essential, nevertheless, for inquiring observers to be on guard against accepting premises philosophically on mere mention and without more ado. It is necessary to be on guard against oversimplification, as well as against undue complication. In any event, we can afford to rest our case for the moment in regard to the foregoing political observations.

What would the experts think of these pages for trying to philosophize politically like this? In particular, what would political leaders with a hard-earned wealth of practical experience think? It is to be hoped that they will think the present argument constructive, as it is intended to be. But, more important, the truth is there for them to discover, each one for himself, as a basis for his own efforts.

The late Henri Bergson, philosopher, member of the French Academy and recipient of the Nobel Prize for Literature, ends with the following thought his challenging work entitled "The Two Sources of Morality and Religion":

"Men do not sufficiently realize that their future is in their own hands. Theirs is the task of determining first of all whether they want to go on living or not. Theirs the responsibility, then, for deciding if they want merely to live, or intend to make just the extra effort required for fulfilling, even on their refractory planet, the essential function of the universe, which is a machine for the making of gods."

What man can imagine, he can do—but without a working knowledge of the benevolent ideal, he lacks the wisdom to operate his part of the whole scheme of existence.

CHAPTER ELEVEN

The Distribution of Wealth

FROM the pages of human experience there are three facts which stand out right away in regard to the subject of inquiry for this chapter. All three are closely inter-related and are now mentioned in no particular order of priority.

One is that the natural design of a distribution of wealth among the members of a community is not merely mechanical nor in terms only of number or of quantity. The design is also qualitative, and specifically related to a system of human reward and punishment.

If it were feasible, all the wealth in the United States could be divided among the citizens one day, on a strictly numerical basis of equality, share and share alike. By the next day, or by the next moment in the ever-changing circumstances of the sequence of events, the distribution would be no longer equal quantitatively, or otherwise. Here we have an example of a natural law which refuses to conform to a man-made order. It is an example of the monotonous kind of distribution that is against human nature.

Qualitatively, a well-principled distribution of wealth within a community is a two-way lane that involves good will in both directions. The good Christian needs to know how to receive as well as to give. Morally, the right policy aim is: from each according to his abilities, to each, not only according to his needs, but *also* according to his deeds.

The second of the facts which emerge so promptly concerns the force of the idea that enters into the act of distribution or, in other words, that concerns the spirit of the deed. A distribution of wealth is always either voluntary or involuntary, willing or coerced.

The fulfillment of a stewardship is the crux of the third fact. Everyone is a steward of wealth in one measure or another. Everyone, himself, either makes use of his authority and lives up to his responsibility or, for some reason, he delegates or relinquishes his authority to another. Within the measure of his freedom of choice and action he can not divest himself of his personal responsibility under the stewardship.

If there were not a final interdependence of individual rights and duties, people would not belong to one and the same dynamic system of thought and deed which embraces all humanity. The working pattern of human life would lack the character of voluntary cooperation essential to its continued existence as an economy.

There are numerous parallels and likenesses to be observed within the framework of stewardship. As another example, there is again the matter of equal justice and equal reward.

If, irrespective of individual performance and accomplishment, every person who entered a contest were sure of receiving a prize and an acclaim equal to the recognition given to every other contestant, there would certainly be a noticeable lack of enthusiasm for making a strenuous effort. Almost no world records, if any of the right kind, are set in a contest where there is no special reward for the winner. It is only within the eternal system of an absolute justice, not in the temporal reckoning alone, that the individual performance of any one can be weighed against his own capabilities as a reliable standard of excellence.

An equal justice does not mean automatically an equal reward. Equal justice means the equality of each person before the law. It means a various reward or a various punishment, in keeping with a loyalty and obedience to a law that applies in common, an individual and personal loyalty and obedience. Except figuratively, it is not the sovereign state that goes to hell, or to heaven. According to an equal justice, it is the individual person, such as you and I. Forever, for the State, is within the bounds of space and time—a framework within which, contrary to much wishful thinking, "the best things in life are *not* free."

How a human plays his hand under the rules of the game is of paramount importance, rather than the particular cards he holds. Nor, in life, can the cards be played entirely, if at all, as a lone hand. The living of a human life is the great example of competitive and, at the same time, mutual stewardship. It is essentially a personal striving for benevolent superiority in which individual talents and handicaps are so designed as to give every entrant an equal opportunity to achieve final success. It is in this sense that "all men are created equal."

The concept of stewardship carries also with it ideas of ownership and property, and there are various forms of wealth. Before we record a few definitions in connection with such terms, we might begin also to think specifically about the opposite characters of two concepts, the Christian and the Marxian. They are different concepts regarding how to go rightly about distributing wealth, as of any given place and time, among the different members of a human community.

A system for the distribution of anything needs a purpose

beyond itself. Hunger is a word of many implications and an idea that is familiar to all. Let us choose, for our present records, some words that illustrate two general, as well as essentially different, approaches to the common problem of distributing wealth in such a manner as to satisfy hunger within a human community.

One is the moral approach which envisages voluntary means of distribution in keeping with individual authority and responsibility under the Christian principle. The other approach is Marxian; it dictates a forced dependence for the individual upon an absolute State, the State as the supreme source of power and the final owner of all wealth. Incidentally, it makes no basic difference if the words which we choose to quote, in illustration, apply to different phases in the respective fulfillment of the contrasting concepts. It is the principle of each concept that is the fundamental issue.

In "The Vision of Sir Launfal," James Russell Lowell has recognized the answer to the essential question—

> " 'The Holy Supper is kept indeed,
> In whatso we share with another's need.
> Not what we give, but what we share—
> For the gift without the giver is bare;
> Who gives himself with his alms feeds three—
> Himself, his hungering neighbor and Me.' "

The poet has expressed in his lines a concept which still waits to be put in force, systematically and explicitly, in terms of governmental aim and policy, although some statutes of ours do make a feeble beginning, incentive-wise, toward the encouragement of personal charitableness as compared with legalistic aid.

Charitableness in action—in other words, actual charity—originates with the individual and can not fulfill entirely its pre-ordained cycle, if personal acquaintanceship and mutual good will be lost along the way. By the same standard, charitableness as an element of private enterprise is the key to an enduring abundance within the political economy.

As to the opposite approach, there is set forth, in the following extract from the *Communist Manifesto*, an open-end list of measures which Marx and Engels recommended as means of speeding the rise of the totalitarian power of the communist, or Soviet Socialist, State, not to say hierarchy. Only the first five or six of the proposed measures are especially pertinent to our subject at hand, but we might as well quote all ten items while we are about it.

"The proletariat," Marx and Engels say in the *Manifesto*, "will use its political supremacy to wrest, by degrees, all capital from the bourgeoisie, to centralise all instruments of production in the hands of the state, i.e., of the proletariat organised as the ruling class; and to increase the total of productive forces as rapidly as possible.

"Of course, in the beginning"—reminiscent, incidentally, of the New Deal in the United States and also, for example, of developments in India today—"this cannot be effected except by means of despotic inroads on the rights of property and on the conditions of bourgeois production; by means of measures, therefore, which appear economically insufficient and untenable, but which, in the course of the movement, outstrip themselves, necessitate further inroads upon the old social order, and are unavoidable as a means of entirely revolutionising the mode of production.

"These measures will of course be different in different countries.

"Nevertheless in the most advanced countries, the following will be pretty generally applicable.

"1. Abolition of property in land and application of all rents of land to public purposes.

"2. A heavy progressive or graduated income tax.

"3. Abolition of all right of inheritance.

"4. Confiscation of the property of all emigrants and rebels.

"5. Centralisation of credit in the hands of the state, by means of a national bank with state capital and an exclusive monopoly.

"6. Centralisation of the means of communication and transport in the hands of the state.

"7. Extension of factories and instruments of production owned by the state; the bringing into cultivation of waste lands, and the improvement of the soil generally in accordance with a common plan.

8. Equal obligation of all to work. Establishment of industrial armies, especially for agriculture.

"9. Combination of agriculture with manufacturing industries; gradual abolition of the distinction between town and country, by a more equable distribution of the population over the country.

"10. Free education for all children in public schools. Abolition of child factory labour in its present form. Combination of education with industrial production, etc."

These ten measures speak for themselves as far as they go. Some speak well but are, nevertheless, misleading. For example, a question arises regarding the last item, namely, the question as to what the children are to be taught in the schools, whether they are to be taught the truth or carefully arranged falsehood.

Wealth, in the physical sense, refers to all material objects having economic utility and to all kinds of property having an exchangeable value, particularly when in the possession of a certain person or group of persons. So the usual definition reads and, analogously, we speak of spiritual and moral possessions.

The root of the word property means "individual" or "belonging to one," and the word "own" has a similar significance. Ownership implies an exclusive right of one as compared to other persons.

Capital is wealth employed in production, or available for productive uses. It is far from being the sinister term that the communists and their fellow travellers make it out to be.

In the economics of the system of gain and loss called capitalism—as generally put into practice in a democratic republic such as our own—the production, distribution and exchange of goods is effected under competitive conditions. It is effected by private enterprise and under private control, subject to the law as duly enacted by the duly elected representatives of the people.

In the system of capitalism, profit is the excess of the price received over the price paid for goods. Goods is another name for merchandise, or wares, or other personal property. Today's capitalism, chastened but yet with much to learn—particularly in regard to the problem of the distribution of wealth—still suffers in reputation on account of the uncharitable record of its less civilized ancestor of the same name.

Labor is the physical or mental service rendered, or the part played, by the worker, or artisan, or operative, in the production of physical things that members of the community like to possess. Such products, among other values, can be included under the general heading of wealth.

A wage is a recompense for services. It is a payment made or received, as the case may be, on account of the performance of labor, physical, mental and spiritual. Human labor is never mechanistic. It is inseparable from the innate faculty of personal decision. By its nature, human deed always comprises two kinds of elements, known to the mind as the material object and the spiritual force.

As opposed to Marxist terms, the foregoing definitions are usual. It would be thoughtless to overlook the power of suggestion which a word can gain persistently through its actual associations. Some words become pleasing, some displeasing. It is largely a matter of education and of experience in one form or another. The meaning of words, such as those spelled out above, can be changed arbitrarily. The associations of a word can be changed deliberately, on paper, for ideological or other purposes, in order to take advantage of relationships already existing in the mind.

In themselves, the above defined concepts remain unaltered by superficial changes, such as a change of label. Shakespeare was right about "a rose by any other name." But the opponents of our capitalistic system of private property and of personally owned enterprise have learned by experience that, concretely, false witness can often take its toll today in the field of political economy as in any other area of the social order.

2.

Speaking of names, there is a Latin word *socius* that means a companion, someone with whom bread is shared—thus someone to go around with or, as the vernacular of France puts it, a *copain*. In English also, the idea which the Latin word stands for is carried forward into such modern terms as sociology and society.

Today the science of sociology deals with the characteristics, the development and the phenomena in general, concerning human relationships within a community, or society.

The English philosopher, Herbert Spencer, whom we have already had occasion to mention, is usually credited with being the chief founder of the modern science of sociology. His life's span was from A.D. 1820 to 1903. As a contemporary of Darwin, he applied the latter's doctrine of evolution to matters of social development.

Spencer's vision is one of rise and fall of community and of empire, the dying out of whatever is unfit on the earth, the survival of that which is fit. But, in line with other materialistic thinking, his philosophy disclaims knowledge of the absolute criterion and, like Natural Selection, is centered in terms of the physical law. His school of thought is, therefore, of only secondary value. His philosophy is on the obvious side, if not always superficial.

It is probable that Herbert Spencer's ideas were influenced in some respects by the so-called positivist philosophy of Auguste Comte, a French thinker, who was Spencer's senior by some twenty years. Comte's philosophy was, in substance, intended to be based directly on human experience only. In his theory of life, humanity itself is the object of its own worship.

Now this does not mean that all modern textbooks on sociology are completely, if at all, positivistic in attitude. But the social concepts of the materialistic age are ordinarily inclined to take sympathetic note of such philosophies as those of Comte and of Spencer, especially when ideas of the kind seem to be harmlessly in the offing. The school of pragmatism, for example, rests on the concept that everything is relative, and only relative, in life. Our present inquiry, on the contrary, fundamentally assumes, and is finding evidence to support the assumption, that the absolute standard of perfection exists and is the real ideal to strive for.

In any case, there are important sociological aspects of

the problem of a right distribution of wealth, aspects that need to be taken always into account.

There are the human wishes for reward, wishes in general and in particular, for personal recognition and security. There are also the human drives away from punishment, such as deprivation, anxiety and monotony, in terms of concrete circumstance. There is the innate desire for personal belongings, or private property, as among the instruments by which an individual is enabled to achieve a perfection of existence.

If actual conditions in the world were absolutely perfect, every good wish and every well-principled human drive would be completely fulfilled, no doubt, as an entirely merited reward. In a state of perfection it can even be imagined— almost—that everyone is everywhere all of the time enjoying everything, at will, in keeping with a perfect choice among alternatives of uniformly superior excellence. There is inherent, in this state, a perfect self-control, in accordance with an absolute knowledge and wisdom in regard to a perfect law and order.

And it is a neat operation indeed, if you can handle it. But on the moral plane a condition of this kind is admittedly, and forever, beyond man's reach in terms of space and time, or as discerned solely by means of the so-called five senses.

Physically, no two objects can occupy the same space at the same time. Change in relative circumstance is continual. Given also the human faculty of choice, no matter how narrow or how wide the field of choice may be, competition is inherent in a society. Competition is a fact and, as such, can be put to right or wrong use.

Francis Hutcheson had some thoughts on subjects of this kind which, especially as Americans, we might now recall. A philosopher born and reared in England, he lived from 1694 to 1746, and worked in Scotland as a professor at the

University of Glasgow during a large part of his career. In the flesh he did not follow his ideas overseas.

Anyhow, he is noted in world history for several of his essays about virtue and beauty, morals and the like, and what interests us particularly is that he put forward, as the criterion of moral action the concept of "the greatest happiness of the greatest number." Jeremy Bentham, English philosopher and political writer, was among those who applied the concept more specifically.

It was an idea which was in line with the revival of classical thought and, in which, there are elements of quality as well as quantity. It is a concept which, in itself, is not entirely reconcilable—it is not fully reconcilable, that is, in terms of the relative alone. But, in a context of absolute perfection, the factors balance up together quite nicely.

Stated in general terms, the concept further serves within a body politic as a useful idea all around, subject, that is, to at least one proviso, an important proviso indeed. It is a good idea as long as it does not lead eventually to putting the cart before the horse so as to think that social justice can be accomplished by legal decree. The Kingdom of Heaven cannot be built primarily by political means.

One of the consequences of Professor Hutcheson's thought is to be found in the American Declaration of Independence, in which Thomas Jefferson penned in due perspective the words "life, liberty and the pursuit of happiness." There is also a second proposition, kindred to Francis Hutcheson's criterion, which has become familiar to American ears. It is a proposition with reference to the spirit of the law of the land, namely, the greatest good of the greatest number—again an excellent proposition, subject to the above proviso.

Neither can we well afford in this inquiry of ours to brush aside age-old ethical concepts, ideas which have apparently perplexed as well as lifted up men's being, since place and time first dawned within his consciousness.

In the calm and beauty of Buddhist thought, as an example, there is to be found the concept that, since all life is as one, the merit of a deed will be in proportion to the degree in which all living things are benefited thereby. All great philosophies seek to resolve the problem of the one as related to the many.

Similiarly, there are the intricacies of ethical thinking on the relationships between the motive and the actual deed and consequence—including the effect of intent, good or evil, as the case may be, on the *doer's* mind, in addition to the effect on the minds of other people. None of this is without its bearing socially and politically, as well as in other ways.

But, when we speak of a well-principled distribution of wealth in a well-inclined social order, what we really mean in these pages is a deliberate and, at the same time, natural distribution of all kinds of wealth in accordance with the Christian principle. "I am come that they might have life and that they might have it more abundantly."

3.

Last year the *Princeton Alumni Weekly* devoted several pages of one of its editions to digests of some of the theses which had been submitted by upperclassmen in the course of their studies at Princeton University. I was interested to notice that one of the theses had dealt with what is commonly known, in the field of political economy, as Say's Law.

In the middle 1930s, Lord Keynes attacked the views of the proponents of Say's Law—and no wonder. Imagine actually centering one's abilities, obligations and resources in the present place and moment and letting nature take its course with a minimum of government interference! A view like that is rank heresy to an ardent Keynesian.

And what is Say's Law? Its substance gives color, for instance, to the idea that the economic system of a nation, such as France, or the United States, or any other, is inherently stable, that depressions or inflations tend "to eliminate themselves within a reasonable period of time," as the above-mentioned digest puts it.

Jean Baptiste Say was a French economist and a writer on various matters of political economy. He lived from 1767 to 1832, and was actively of Adam Smith's school of thought, which is definitely inclined toward the capitalistic system. In fact, the record tells us that he popularized a number of the ideas contained in Adam Smith's historic book, "An Inquiry Into the Nature and the Causes of the Wealth of Nations."

Say's theory of markets and his concept of the entrepreneur extended, and further integrated, Smith's theories of free enterprise and free trade, foreign as well as domestic, not that any particular economic theories have ever turned out to be perfect in practice.

In spite of his reiterated belief in the worth of capitalism, Lord Keynes, 1st baron of Tilton—the Right Honorable John Maynard Keynes (1883-1946), economist and monetary expert, whom this volume has mentioned not too sympathetically from time to time—departed increasingly during his later years from his earlier classical ideas. From favoring so-called free enterprise, his expressed views turned toward a controlled economy, and not only so as a temporary matter of expediency.

He expressly favored, that is, an economy controlled by government fiat, rather than by natural law, in case a choice had to be made between the two. If the government were of a democratic character, so much the better, but man-made controls were to be the thing in either event.

If we were to listen only to the proponents of a "controlled economy," which is another way of saying the proponents of a usually unnecessary loss of personal freedom, we might think that there is no choice other than between inflexible controls and extremes of *laissez-faire*. But there is another alternative. The truth is that every moment there is a happy medium in matters of practice and procedure in the light of the benevolent ideal. And the happy medium is not always to be found in "the middle of the road," not in the middle of some roads. It depends.

In everyday affairs, there can be actual conditions of emergency, in which an economy needs to be under a high degree of government control in spite of a normal and long range objective that is contrary to such control. The ideal of a minimum of governmental dictation may well remain unchanged. It is also true that stability is a characteristic of the well-balanced trend. But amid ever-changing circumstance no economic doctrine can afford to be too inflexible or intemperate.

There is no economic panacea for human ills. Economics is only a part of the design for human being which, in whole and in part, is governed integrally by a law that is above human power to change. The right approach is from the standpoint that there are general laws of nature, general rules of morality which apply in the fields of economics, sociology and politics as thoroughly as elsewhere. They are general rules in terms of an over-all equilibrium, inclined toward a common aim of collective perfection.

These are only big words, if you like. Nevertheless, in addition to the matter of reward, there are penalties for economic mistakes, as for human mistakes of other kinds.

Consider Say's Law, for instance, on the assumption that it is practically in accord with natural law. Or consider the law that a country must always be careful to look continually to its own equilibrium in order to be able to help other countries in a good cause. A law like either of these can be blocked, thwarted and delayed temporarily in its operation but it can not be changed fundamentally, nor obliterated, nor broken with impunity.

If blocked by man-made regulation, natural law finally has its way—accompanied by a degree of violent readjustment that varies with the character and the extent of the lack of true balance to be set aright. And the lasting remedy is through education, or by the hard way of re-education, not only in regard to the physical law of nature, but also in regard to the spiritual law. As of today, the outlook for the world would be grim indeed, if there were only materialistic means of righting the present state of world disequilibrium.

We come, then, to look specifically into an element of our theory already frequently referred to, into education as a key to a willing loyalty and obedience to "the Laws of Nature, and of Nature's God." It is an element always of topmost priority in a moral order of first things first.

CHAPTER TWELVE

Education and Willingness

"For if the trumpet shall give an uncertain
sound, who shall prepare himself to the battle?"
I CORINTHIANS 14:8

THE late John Dewey, we may now recall, in addition
to our previous mention of him, was not only a force
in the "progressive school movement," but was also the
originator of a utilitarian brand of philosophy known as
instrumentalism.

This philosophy of his, akin to the pragmatic school of
thought, maintains that there is only a relative kind of truth
in human being. Thought itself is considered to be probably
no more than some kind of instrument of the body, an
implement developed by the physical organism as a means
of adjusting itself in life to an ever-changing environment
of space and time. We have marked already this kind of
rationalization in regard to thinking. It is an hypothesis
which is contrary to our own theory of the nature of
thought.

Instrumentalism agrees well with the scheme of materialistic determinism. In it there is no absolute good in which
to have an inspiring faith. There is no real place in such

philosophy for the rôle of the abstract ideal nor for the saving grace of a vicarious atonement. Experimentalism is the thing. One tension leads to another, with no real hope of recognizing a right balance, even if, according to Professor Dewey, there were such a condition to be found.

For the human being, the agnostic views of instrumentalism are, then, particularly open to demoralizing influences. Like all the ill-centered hypotheses, astronomical and other, which have been accepted from time to time in the course of human trial and error, the concept of our being naturally in the dark without any changeless light to guide by, tends to compound confusion and, within the limits of its acceptance, to lead from bad to worse.

Some months ago I read of an incident in John Dewey's career that impressed me as particularly significant in regard to the character of his thinking. While teaching at Columbia, he (Professor Dewey) was asked by a young man in one of his classes, "Is there a purpose in the universe?" John Dewey replied, "This is a question we do not ask in this course."

And the narrative adds that "the young man came away saying, 'But that is the question I ask.'"

From its first page to its last, this book is concerned with the same question the young man asked of Professor Dewey. Likewise, it is even more concerned with the answer, and especially so in this chapter on education.

To direct the young man's question toward the particular subject of the present pages: Is there a universal purpose in education? Does the nature of human existence, discernible as its working pattern is, indicate that there is inherently a general purpose in education, a purpose paramount to all other aims in the educational field?

Well, no matter in what terms they be stated, these are far from being new questions. It is likely that members of the human race have been puzzling over the subject for a long while indeed.

Technically, education is a "leading forth," as indicated by the roots of the word, and the process is associated particularly with a leading forth of the young. Traditionally, and also with good reason, the best place to begin the education of the young is in the well-principled home. For the true home is the altar and the stronghold of the family, and the family, in turn, is the unit of a well-ordered society.

In principle, there is no conflict but, instead, a mutual support to be found in the unique potentiality of the home as compared with the vital rôle of the school of the outside world, be the formal teachings of the latter directly under either lay or religious control.

More useful as the starting point of our continuing inquiry, however, is the fact that education has to do with thought. It concerns the thinking of every human being, young and old. It is not a process of leading, and of being led, in some aimless fashion. Rather, it is, or is destined to be, a well-defined process by which a mind is influenced—led, not driven against its will—to accept an idea as true.

And an important process it is when we stop to consider that, individually, we get out of the mind the thoughts, and only the thoughts, which the mind has in it. It is in the general thought and in the particular idea, as grasped by the mind, that the cycle of actual fulfillment originates.

"In the beginning was the Word," Saint John tells us. "Word" is a translation of the Greek *logos,* the meaning of which, aside from theological interpretations, can be extended to include the concept that inspires the spoken word itself. To neglect the concept, or the thought, is to neglect the substance and its origin.

Lenin, among others, was right, only too right, about thinking things through with care, even though his own thinking failed to go far enough to recognize the whole truth. For it is not the bare fact of the existence of a concept, instead it is the character and the use of the concept, which are of ultimate importance to the outcome of human affairs.

"Be yourself" is questionable advice. The character of a person is modified currently by the thoughts which he has really accepted as true. Be careful of your ideals and of your ideas is more to the point than "be yourself." Be careful of the quality of the ideals and be careful of the nature of the ideas which you accept to become part of yourself. Education alone is not enough to insure good character. It can influence, but not take the place of, personal decision.

To get back to the twofold question which we posed ourselves a few paragraphs ago, it is possible, as well as desirable, to avoid the treadmill of endlessly relative thinking in considering the answer.

In the foregoing pages, we have considered the absolute nature of the principle of human existence. In the scheme, the pattern and the system of opposites which we refer to as human life, we have noted that the integration and the application of human strengths, religious, political and otherwise, are finally governed by changeless law, that absolute principle is the saving grace of relativity.

We have recognized that the individual person is the unit of mankind, that without the individual member there would be no community on the earth.

Every one of the elements of the truth which we have rediscovered for ourselves, during the present search, indicates that there is an absolute answer to our twofold question. In fact, the answer itself is already set forth at the end of the preceding chapter. There is a universal purpose in education, a purpose paramount to every other. There are many ways of expressing it. The purpose is, finally, that every human being have as complete a knowledge as possible of God's laws, the laws of existence, and have the wisdom to obey His laws willingly.

On the moral plane of the community we can also say, in keeping with the final aim of perfection, that the paramount purpose of education is to help the human being to tell right clearly from wrong, and, so, to act willingly and most effectively in the good cause.

A human being is nearly always willing, if not always able, to do what he thinks is right—right according to the ideals of the moral standards which he has accepted subjectively as comprising the truth. But even more important from the standpoint of education, and also of human sovereignty, is the condition that results when a human's belief as to what is right is also the real truth. For that believer, and for a community made up of like believers, wisdom, faith and willingness tend to coincide. It is potentially, if not yet actually, an almost invincible combination.

Accordingly, one of the primary responsibilities of a benevolent sovereignty relates to education. One of the primary functions of education is to support and strengthen a benevolent rule. And these relationships are of special concern and importance in a sovereignty such as that of the United States, which relies for its continued progress in the right direction upon the actual wisdom of the persons who comprise the body politic.

There is much ado these days about freedom of thought in education and about letting nearly anyone with so-called liberal ideas teach nearly anything he wants to teach. Such ado is likely to cover up a big mistake, a mistake which must please, if it be not actually fostered by, the enemies of the Christian spirit in which our government was conceived.

The design of existence is to let each human being learn for himself as well as to choose for himself—within bounds of natural law. Achievement, including old-fashioned salvation, is finally personal. And, at the same time, the framework of life for humanity is one of mutual interest, responsibility and helpfulness—within a proper discipline.

In the individual human life and in the social order, the ideal condition is one of self-discipline on the part of each of the members, of self-direction under the guidance of the ideals which the law implies. Herein lies a right answer, for example, to such dire prediction as that of Mr. Malthus, about the over-crowded future of the human race. No person is free to do entirely as he pleases. As far as nature is concerned, no one is a law unto himself.

The opposite sides and the contrasting aspects of any worthwhile subject need to be pointed out carefully in education. There needs to be freedom of debate and of individual expression of opinion. But all human beings, and particularly the young, need an educational leadership which is certain of the right direction in general, a leadership which leaves no breach between religious and political thinking, no doubt as to the essential difference between good and evil.

No wonder there is sometimes the urge to get out of school. Even education has to be justified by a purpose above and beyond itself. It is not in the act of teaching, but in the teaching of the truth for a great purpose that education fully justifies itself. On the moral plane, there is need for good leadership, and only good leadership, in education, as in every other field.

Good leadership seeks cooperation—under a discipline in common. Its aim is not coërcion, one by another, not a coërcion of thought, even though it is necessary to use physical force to maintain law and order under which to teach.

Moreover, beyond a critical point of ill-balance or disaster —a point which, in principle, concerns every member of humanity—human thinking cannot be coerced, or otherwise led, into a belief which is contrary to the everlasting truth. In spite, even, of good personal intention, education contrary to the truth is either an actual or an attempted coërcion of the human being.

In one of his books, entitled "The Use of Life," the late Sir John Lubbock, British banker, member of Parliament, author and man of science—he and Charles Darwin were close friends —touches on some aspects of the present subject. He has the following to say, in quoting the English historian, Edward Gibbon:

"Education is the harmonious development of all our faculties. It begins in the nursery and goes on at school but does not end there. It continues through life, whether we will or not. . . . 'Every person,' says Gibbon, 'has two educations, one which he receives from others, and one, more important, which he gives himself.' "

It seems certain that we can go along voluntarily with the above views of these gentlemen. We can agree with them, provided that, at the beginning of the present age, we be allowed to call attention also to a third kind of education, namely, to the leading forth which comes from the flashes of the truth by which, from time to time, the magnificence of eternal thought reveals itself directly to the minds of men.

2.

An immensely important element of the community is made up of those members who are devoting the work of a lifetime to problems of education. The present author is not among the number who can lay claim to their greatness. His experience has been that of one taught, not one who teaches. This book is only in a position to observe, and to make a choice within its limitations.

It is one thing to read, in an article in the American Legion Magazine regarding one of the colleges of Columbia University that:

"With 100,000 alumni TC has managed to seat about one-third of the presidents or deans now in office at accredited U. S. teacher training schools. Its graduates make up about 20 per cent of all our public school teachers. Over a fourth of the superintendents of schools in the 168 U. S. cities with at least 50,000 population are TC-trained. Roughly 84,000,-000 people live in those cities. Their children—*your* children —to the number of a good 10,000,000 are thus, from nine to three, each day under the influence of Teachers College, Columbia University."

It is another thing to bring home to oneself the importance of the character of the philosophy with which education at Teachers College, Broadway and 120th Street, New York City, is imbued.

And, for example, what is the unifying philosophy, or the determining, ideological standard of perfection, at TC, as of this moment? Is it friendly, or is it antagonistic, to the spirit upon which the United States Constitution depends for its integrity and effectiveness? Whatever the answer may be, the influence of such an important institution as Teachers College is, in itself, enough to highlight one of the indispensable projects for the members of an enduringly benevolent body politic. The project is, namely, for such members to keep in touch carefully and continually with the substance of what goes on around them in formal sources of education, to keep informed in order to act rightly as needed.

Education can be classified as formal or informal, general

or specialized, elementary or advanced, public or private, sectarian or nonsectarian, military or civilian, and so on.

From the earliest teachings to today's learning, from the ancient school of Socratic thought, with its inquiry into general truth and virtue, to the modern exposition of Pavlov's "conditioned reflexes," there have been many processes that have gone under the heading of education in one sense, or another. The various aspects represent a particularly tempting group of islands for exploration but, in view of the above-mentioned limitations, it is better this time that our party stick close to the mainland.

Even so, there is more than enough for us to observe. For instance, there is again the matter of words, or of the association of words with ideas, a device which can be put to good use, or the contrary. It is a matter that involves, not only varying contrasts between ideals and actualities—and, therefore, the emotions, too—but also that involves actual techniques of education, of propaganda, advertising, salesmanship, or whatever the particular area of interest of the moment may be called.

An association of ideas is a subject of high consequence in personal and community affairs of every kind, not omitting politics and religion. There is, for instance, the word "united," a word which has excellent associations in the mind of the American patriot. This is a word which we should consider more fully later on.

And there are such words as liberty, democracy and peace, which are likewise dear to most American hearts as are also symbols, such as the cross and the flag. In such associations, however, it is necessary to be continually on guard. For the process of identifying a word with a particular idea can be used in the wrong direction. The process can be turned into a destructive technique.

Some time ago we noted a question in regard to sincerity. It had to do with whether, or not, sincerity alone is sufficient to justify itself. We can now say more confidently that it depends. As an abstract quality sincerity, like honesty, is virtuous. But, concretely, if sincerity be taken to mean "desirous of conforming to the truth," then the actual justification of sincerity depends on whether the accepted truth be really true, or be falsehood mistaken for the truth. A sincerely misguided person is a menace of the formidable kind.

Words are vehicles, usually identified with, and possessed jointly by, a number of ideas. The vehicle carries the ideas, their armor and their other belongings. Sometimes a strange character, such as a bad idea in disguise, sneaks into the vehicle just for the ride or, much more likely, to use the good front for untoward purposes.

Take words like those just mentioned, a word like democracy, or take combinations of words such as "civil rights" and "freedom of speech." All of these terms, for example, have gained excellent associations in the United States. But the character of the active sponsorship of a word can change almost imperceptibly, for better or for worse. The possession of a word is never in changeless hands in the sequence of events in the world. Such agreeable names as the "Welfare State" and the "well-planned economy" now serve as cover only too often for steps toward extreme socialism and communism itself.

The word democracy stems simply from the Greek word *demos* which pertained to the districts of the city of Athens, and so the word came to imply the free choice of the people, by districts. But the centralized authority of a State can use the word for an opposite purpose.

When an evil government, within a nation, for example, has to be overcome by benevolent forces from outside— overcome, at first, by force of arms—there is a well-principled rule to follow, as a matter of high policy. As a rule, it is better to aid the good elements among the nationals of the country to gain, or to regain, an effective sovereignty therein, rather than for a foreign power, as such, to invade the country. The rule is, further, that an occupation of one country by the forces of another should last no longer than the situation really requires, for its trend to be truly and firmly established toward the right ideals. This is apropos of the carefully planned and misleading associations, plus the unfriendly implications, in the slogan of the communists that "the U.S.S.R. is too large a territory for any other nation, or nations, to conquer and to occupy."

Liberty and liberal come from the Latin vehicle for the idea of personal freedom. Those opposed to the development of such freedom can use the word in disguise to mean the freedom of the State from personal restraint.

The word peace is also a peculiarly important vehicle. It seems to be associated, in the American mind, mostly with a detached state of perfection, whereas, realistically, it is an end result of many aims and policies. This is a word which we need especially to think about during our remaining pages.

As far as education is concerned, however, the aspect of association which seems most to be of interest now refers again to ideals, actualities and emotions. When events and actualities trend perceptibly toward the fulfillment of a cherished ideal, the emotional reaction tends to be agreeable. Hope has proved to be worthwhile. Faith and perseverance have brought reward. Happiness is the order of the day. But when an ideal is violated, or desecrated, or the trend is in that direction, when the fulfillment of an ideal has been frustrated, then sorrow, anger or similar emotional tensions naturally arise.

If everything in life were currently and finally relative,

nothing would make much difference at all. There would be little, if any, current of moral energy to light the signals of the emotions which are so important a part of man's equipment for his journey through the world.

The emotions are primarily mental reactions or processes. They are reactions to an agreement, or to a disagreement, as the case may be, between the ideal and the actual or presumed accomplishment, condition or event. Emotional reactions or processes always involve an ideal, be it a part of the native endowment or later acquired.

Thus, from the beginning and throughout the life of anyone, it is important for him to possess good ideals, so that the right kind of ideas and consequences will please and encourage him when they should, and so that he will get angry when, and only when, it is right to do so. Righteous indignation as well as due thankfulness, aroused emotions intense enough to result in corrective action without unnecessary delay, are essential to the progress of society toward perfection.

The role of education includes, therefore, not only the teaching of relative platitudes, but the human being needs also to be led forth to recognize the absolute ideal as clearly as he does the brightest star. The mission of education is not only to teach the truth, but also to teach the truth enthusiastically.

In life, the conflict between good and evil, between perfect and imperfect existence, is continual. "If the trumpet shall give an uncertain sound?"—this has been a good question for hundreds and thousands of years.

CHAPTER THIRTEEN

On Nations' Being United

"Only the Spirit, if it breathe upon the clay, can create Man."

ANTOINE DE SAINT EXUPÉRY
Wind, Sand and Stars

FOR two or more sovereign powers to be as one is a different proposition from their having agreed to support together any number of high-sounding phrases. Nations can be truly allied politically, by implementing in unison their supreme ideals. They can become truly allied, that is, if their ideals are united in principle. They can work well and lastingly together if, and only if, their ideals are of one and the same nature.

The American people like the word "united." It is a word that has excellent associations in the minds of nearly all citizens of the United States. It makes us think of our own union of states. It leads us to wish that all of the various people in the world could enjoy a similar union. It recalls agreeably our Pledge of Allegiance to the Flag:

"I pledge allegiance to the flag of the United States of America and to the Republic for which it stands, one nation under God, indivisible, with liberty and justice for all."

If the present "United Nations," or any comparable body

179

of the past or future, is to be viewed realistically, however, it is necessary not to be thrown off our guard by the mere appearance of the word "united" in its official name. On the contrary, it is of the utmost importance to identify carefully and truthfully the good and the bad elements of the organization in question, independently of its name.

From the standpoint of achieving a continually better life for one and all, all human interest and responsibility is essentially mutual. But, given the collectivist propaganda that is passed from person to person these days, it becomes fairly easy to fall into a habit of thinking also that practically everyone in the world is now almost like everyone else, that what is just is always equal. Nothing could be much further from fact, except, perhaps, some of the current notions regarding the political significance of "one."

Our observations at the moment concern especially the present UN, its Charter and its "Universal Declaration of Human Rights." Consider first some favorable aspects.

Among the comparatively good, if unofficial, features of the organization in question, there are the well-intentioned ideals of world peace and of justice for all men that have actuated, and that continue to actuate, so many of the representatives of the traditionally well-principled governments which, among others, have subscribed to the Charter of the organization. Too much good will has gone into the formation and the operation of the present UN for it to be condemned carelessly and without sufficient cause.

In the credit column there is also the faculty of the UN to serve as a convenient and powerful world forum.

As of potential, if not of immediate, benefit there is the actual experience which has been gained through conscientious effort in the UN, experience which has, nevertheless, been gained largely at a tragic cost of lives. The rule is that human experience, as likewise man-made instruments such as the UN forum, can be put to either right or wrong use in the community.

To view further the less bright, not to say the darker side, the protagonists of the "United Nations" are seeking to have us believe that the UN as now constituted is an organization indispensable to a peacefully regulated order of international politics. However, a political vacuum in the field of such desirable international affairs would *not* result for the well-principled nations of the world in case the ties of the present UN organization were dissolved.

Too often we are led to think that we are faced with a choice solely between the present UN and no international body at all. Such an idea is not the truth. The UN has no just right to a monopoly. Moreover, alternative arrangements and other forums are actually available. For example, even though their respective existences now seem at times to be menaced by difficulties and dangers, the North Atlantic Treaty Organization—NATO—and similar treaty organizations in the Pacific areas and elsewhere offer a true basis and a real hope for effective coöperation among all benevolently inclined nations in the world.

A name such as Allied Nations, not United Nations, points to terms of reference that make good sense at today's stage of political evolution and within the foreseeable future, at least insofar as the world as a whole be concerned. As of a given place and time, the right degree of political alliance, or of federal union, between sovereign powers depends partly on factors which are far from being changeless, and also far from being as one, in the course of human events.

It is public knowledge that there are two opposing blocs of nations in the UN. One is the communist bloc of nations. The other bloc is comprised of the nations of the free, or non-communist, world. That fact is clear and widely known. But the special nature of the opposition between the two blocs does not seem to be so distinctly recognized. The opposition is of a kind that is irreconcilable.

With the principle of our own government before us as an example, we are reasonably familiar, in general, with the ideals of the sovereign powers which stand up to be counted on the side of human freedom under God's laws. On the opposite side are the national governments responsive to the atheist concept as implemented in the Soviet Socialist State and as now centered in the Kremlin, not to mention Peiping.

One way to view the aim and policy of the atheistic bloc is to consider the Communist Party and, in particular, the guiding concept of International Communism. This book does not accept a defeatist attitude toward communism. It believes that communism is wrong in principle and, therefore, essentially weak. But that does not mean that a knowledge of present facts and current events is to be neglected.

The U. S. S. R. Constitution of 1936, as also the Soviet agreements at Yalta and at Potsdam—and the agreement in San Francisco in regard to the UN Charter—are, in reality, instruments of the Communist Party, whatever else they may also be. And they are godless instruments if there ever were any.

Moreover, it is a fair assumption, from the daily evidence, that a carefully trained and experienced panel of experts in, or of, the Kremlin have concentrated their efforts, at one time or another, if not continually, on figuring out techniques as well as alternative aims and policies, whereby to achieve key objectives of the Party. This means, at the same time, for achieving the aims of the Union of Soviet Socialist Republics, as the mainstay of the intended Communist Universal State.

Our own explorings in the direction of the Communist

Party, however, can now be brief. For purposes of the record we can make reference to a portion of a speech made by Secretary of State Dulles, of the United States, at a recent Inter-American Conference held at Caracas, Venezuela.

"International Communism," the Secretary said, "is that far-flung clandestine political organization which is operated by the leaders of the Communist Party of the Soviet Union. Since 1939, it has brought 15 once independent nations into a state of abject servitude. It has a hard core of agents in practically every country of the world. The total constitutes not a theory, not a doctrine, but an aggressive, tough, political force, backed by great resources, and serving the most ruthless empire of modern times.

"Most of the leaders of the Soviet Communist Party appear before the eyes of the world as responsible officials of the Soviet government. In this capacity they conduct relations with the other governments thru the traditional institutions of diplomacy. But at the same time they operate and control this world-wide clandestine political organization to which I have referred.

"Until the Second World War, Moscow's control over this organization was exercised openly thru the central headquarters of the Communist International, the so-called 'Comintern.' That was a political association to which all of the Communist parties belonged, and it had its seat in Moscow. During the war the Comintern was officially abolished. Since that time the control over the foreign Communist parties has been exercised by the Moscow leaders secretly and informally, but for the most part no less effectively than before . . .

"The disciplinary requirements include a firm insistence that loyalty to the movement—which means in effect loyalty to the leaders of the Communist Party of the Soviet Union —shall take precedence over every other obligation including love of country, obligation to family, and the honor of one's own personal conduct. . . . The overall purpose for which this organization is maintained and operated is to act as an instrument for the advancement of the world-wide political aims of the dominant group of Moscow leaders.

"This, then, is the answer to 'What is international communism?' "

As far as this chapter of ours is concerned, however, the background throughout is the sad plight of the well-intentioned nation that wants to be united in a friendly fashion with practically all other nations, right away, and almost no matter what the truth may be. Neglected is the fact that unity, for unity's sake alone, is not a good enough reason.

Or, in origin, it is the plight of the individual human who is inclined to believe that it is possible for governments to become united, no matter that they be inspired respectively by ideals of opposite principle.

How easily seems to have been forgotten in a generation or two, President Lincoln's reminder of the Biblical wisdom that a house divided against itself cannot stand.

2.

Part of Article VI of the United States Constitution provides as follows:

"This Constitution and the laws of the United States which shall be made in pursuance thereof and all treaties made, or which shall be made, under the authority of the United States, shall be the supreme law of the land, and the judges in every State shall be bound thereby, anything in the Constitution or laws of any State to the contrary notwithstanding."

Adherence by the United States and by other member nations to the Charter of the "United Nations" is by *treaty*.

So, within itself, the supreme law of our land is faced with the problem of reconciling laws which are irreconcilable by their very natures. No moral ground is left for compromise. And the decisions of the Supreme Court of the United States in interpretation of the law take on an added significance of far reaching importance, in view of the conflicting ideologies involved through the treaty agreement in question.

In the rise of civilization, political law has come to recognize various rights and duties of the individual and of the community, within the legal framework of a governmental exercise of sovereign power. The United States Government is essentially a government by law, not by person. Nevertheless, the personal beliefs of those in high positions of governmental authority and responsibility, such as in the Supreme Court, are of great influence. It is of fundamental importance that their beliefs be truly right, that their ideals be in favor of the original spirit of the Constitution and that, accordingly, their decisions, for naturally moral reasons, be against the highly centralized and overwhelmingly powerful State. Political law is just when it conforms to the natural law of morality, otherwise not.

As a nation we believe in the original and final goodness of God's natural law—be the law in the form of physical or spiritual law, or of a moral law which combines the two to constitute the laws of human nature on the Earth—or we do not so believe. In this basic issue an individual, or a nation, is either for or against. There is no room for the halfway of complacency, UN or no UN.

And even that fact is not enough to insure clarity politically. The principle points to a corresponding ideal with respect to sovereign aim and governmental system. The actual ideal also needs to be identified, and followed systematically by the members of the body politic.

The United States Constitution provides for a government as nearly in keeping with God's natural scheme and pattern for the system of human society as the Founding Fathers could arrange for the United States Government to be. It is of infinite importance that this fact be associated, in the thinking of all members of our nation, with the innumerable blessings and benefits which have accrued accordingly to American citizens, themselves, and also to other people.

The American Declaration of Independence makes due reference to Divine Providence and to the laws of the Creator. The United States Constitution was "Done in convention by the unanimous consent of the States present the 17th day of September in the year of Our Lord 1787." But the basic documents of the prayerless "United Nations" make no mention whatsoever of any authority higher than political power. The Assembly rules may have come to permit a minute of silence for personal thoughts at the opening of a plenary meeting, but the spoken word of prayer, the song of worship in unison, is banned officially.

The Charter of the UN and its companion papers have much to say about human dignity, but nothing to say about a worshipful belief in God. They neglect, completely, the original and final source of personal strengths, and represent a logical extreme of humanism—an extreme, because the humanist movement did not set out to join forces with atheism, but, on the contrary, to foster the true humanities of classical learning and the further ingredients of enlightenment that are known as the liberal arts.

And, unhappily, it is not only such utterances as those contained in the UN Charter that reflect the self-satisfied brand of atheistic thought. A trend of thinking in that idolatrous direction has grown to alarming proportions in the human community during the later years of the so-called scientific age. Human dignity is by way of becoming the Golden Calf of our day.

Not that there is anything wrong with human dignity, or worthiness, in its right context and perspective. The individual human being, the body, mind and soul indivisible, is the unit of human life without which humanity, as we know it, would not exist. From ancient struggles against tyranny onward to Magna Charta and to the United States Constitution, men have won such worthy rights as private property, *habeas corpus* and trial by jury. They have won acceptance of such principles as equal justice before the law and the inviolability of the home.

But this does not mean that human dignity is self-sufficient or an ultimate source of strength. Human being has to have a purpose as well as an origin beyond itself, in order to justify its difficult enough existence.

"Every man a King," "I am a law unto myself," "This above all, to thine own self be true," "Nothing is either good nor bad, and only thinking makes it so"—here are expressions to beware of, except in due context. Or think, for instance, about the "unconquerable soul" of Henley's eloquent, but considerably benighted poem, *Invictus*.

Out of proper perspective, such concepts of personal importance can but lead in the direction of political formulas for bitterness and strife. Such ideas favor a confusion that invites tyranny. The human universe itself could hardly be expected to operate for long, if it tried to be centered separately in each individual human will, no matter how relatively good each of such wills might be as of a given place and time.

Over-developed individualism at one extreme. Over-developed collectivism at the other extreme. Action and reaction. The political pendulum swings haltingly back and forth, and it is only by means of changeless standards of perfection, only by reference to the absolute, that the right and dutiful course between the extremes can be safely charted by the individual and, in turn, by the nation.

Therefore, as Dostoyevsky, great Russian novelist of pre-Lenin days, has pointed out in "The Brothers Karamazov"—and his thought supports more than the political argument—

"Even those who have renounced Christianity and attack it, in their utmost being still follow the Christian ideal, for hitherto neither their subtlety nor the ardor of their hearts has been able to create a higher ideal of man and of virtue than the ideal given by Christ of old. When it has been attempted, the result has been only grotesque."

3.

A few years ago—in December 1948, to be more exact—a "Universal Declaration of Human Rights" was proclaimed by the General Assembly of the "United Nations." American officials were among those who participated actively in the formulation of the ideas and in the preparation of the text.

This so-called Universal Declaration includes, in its text, parts of a number of phrases which appear in the American Declaration of Independence. It includes also a few samples of wording taken from the original ten Amendments to the United States Constitution, which, together, are known as our Bill of Rights. But the similarity ends with the words and the alphabetical letters of the phrases. Again there is the all-pervading difference in principle which we are further to note elsewhere in this chapter.

It is in its Universal Declaration of Human Rights that the UN really gives itself away in the matter of intent. The Charter of the UN, although full of double-talk, like the

Soviet Constitution of 1936, is not as openly Marxian as is the Universal Declaration.

The evidence is that, contrary to the assumptions of unwary advocates of the UN, the intent of the Universal Declaration is, initially, to make "despotic inroads" upon personal property and to inject seeds of state socialism into the present system of private enterprise in the United States and like-principled countries. The intent is, finally, to overthrow the political system of individual freedom under natural law and to usher in the Universal Soviet Socialist State.

In other words, measures which tend toward confusion, unrest and conflict, specifically in the non-communist nations, are sponsored wittingly, or unwittingly, by the members of the UN—"measures which appear economically insufficient but which in the course of the movement outstrip themselves and necessitate further inroads upon the old social order." They are measures which lead to the temptation to give in to ill-principled constraints for the sake of immediate, though unjust and fleeting, material gain and to pass along to someone else the day of reckoning.

The Universal Declaration, atheistic as it is, proceeds on the proposition, and is, in fact, dedicated to the proposition, that human rights are gifts of the State. It declares and sets forth arbitrary wishes as though they were inborn rights politically. Thus centered, it holds out promises that are un-natural and that, accordingly, lead toward personal frustrations and the kind of social tensions that turn citizen against citizen.

As a means of weakening the financial resources of private industry, of distorting the profit incentive and of increasing reliance on the powers of the State, the ideology embodied in the UN gives rise to pressures, for instance, on manufacturers and other business concerns for guarantees of material security, present and future, to practically one and all on the payroll, employe and official. The UN ideology presses for guarantees against economic risks which, sooner or later, are beyond such guaranteeing within the changeless scheme and pattern that requires ever-changing, material circumstance.

All 30 of the Articles of the Universal Declaration should be read and considered, not only separately, but also as a whole. Throughout the document, fine words about freedoms are mixed with tested seeds of discord. The Universal Declaration is not the confused document of high ideal which, at first, it may seem to be. On the contrary, it is a document which has been "carefully thought out" in intent and for application as an instrument of human oppression of the many by a select minority.

To quote from an introductory paragraph of the Universal Declaration, the "United Nations" would "strive by teaching and education to promote respect for these rights and freedoms and by progressive measures national and international to secure their universal and effective recognition and observation both among the peoples of the Member States and among the peoples under their jurisdiction."

Thus, the document in question is of urgent concern to the patriotic citizen who would care to realize more fully what he is up against politically, as well as educationally, these days.

In general, not to mention problems in particular, he and his thinking are up against continual, wedge-like pressures and carefully applied leverages from and by the proponents of the Universal Soviet Socialist Atheistic State. The pressures and the leverages are directed at any areas of weakness, physical or spiritual, which the communists and their fellow travellers, the state socialists, can detect within the ranks of their opponents.

4.

The use of the word "united" tended to put the UN organization off to a good start in the thoughts of many a trustful American patriot. But the "United Nations" are no more truly united than the U.S.A. is with the U.S.S.R. The UN has been operating under false pretenses ever since the beginning of its existence. Behind the facade of such good works as the UN Children's Fund and the World Court at The Hague—both of which, for instance, could well operate under auspices other than UN—destructive propaganda is advancing apace. At least, such is the case in the United States.

Human emotions are stirred to take corrective action when events trend suddenly or persistently away from cherished ideals. For the United States, the force of UN teaching represents a violation of the original ideals of our Republic. But the truth in regard to the trend has been well disguised, while the UN has been trying to change our accepted ideals, and to bring about the reversals of opinion which are necessary in advance thereof. It has been disguised by means of carefully planned associations between word and mental images, and by various other means of infiltrating the domain of the mind where ideas are either accepted as being true, or rejected as being false.

In order to illustrate some of our findings so far, we might well devote the remainder of our observations on nations' being united, to the subject of actual infiltration. Also, we ourselves might try to do a little associating of ideas.

It is relatively easy to figure out where an infiltration of the ultra-socialist and anti-religious ideas, which combine in communism, would be especially effective in the body politic of a democratic republic, such as our own. Our love of human freedom has led us, however, into an habitual lack of due diligence against the inroad of demoralizing ideas and slogans into our current thinking and deep into our minds.

Among the key places for infiltration, according to communist strategy for the domination of thought and, in turn, of action, we can note, in general—aside, that is, from either praise or adverse criticism of actual personnel and personalities—such influential organizations and activities as schools, colleges and universities; libraries, books, book publishing and book reviews; art and decoration; newspapers, magazines and similar publications; stage and screen; radio broadcasts and other instruments of world-wide communication; and, more recently, television. Churches and other religious organizations are fields of immense importance. So are youth groups in particular. And there are the philanthropic foundations, with large financial means available for special projects.

Likewise, among the indicated places, there are executive and other strategic and tactical positions in business and industrial management and, comparably, in labor unions. Although, for the moment, the latter are of more importance to the communists from the standpoint, for instance, of interrupted industrial production and of numerical strength politically, both private employer and labor union are slated for drastic control or outright liquidation in due course, according to the Soviet scheme and pattern.

And, as of high priority, there are also the political parties and the Government itself, with its civilian branches and its military establishment. Governmental posts can exert a direct influence on policies of State and on measures of action, domestic and foreign.

By the spoken and written slogan, by the appealing pamphlet and poster, by the artistic symbol, communism in disguise is wedging itself into many a mind among us and, in no small degree, via the UN. Through distortions of definition, through repeated association of words and persons with already agreeable or disagreeable ideas and objects, through appeals to the half-truth, through the big lie, through flattery and overemphasis of self-importance, through neglect, ridicule and blurring of religious principle and worship — through these, among other techniques, the enemies of our principle of government and of our political institutions have managed to confuse our thinking, as a nation. In consequence, they have led us, as a nation, to weaken our current ability to act rightly.

For the reasons above observed and recorded, the flag of the "United Nations" should be a danger signal for us. Not without just cause is it referred to sometimes as the "spider web" flag of the UN. The web of crisscross lines of latitude and longitude that appear on the UN emblem are, by coincidence, symbolic enough in an unintended way.

As another association, a likeness of the Trojan Horse might be used to stand for the UN, but it would be unfair to the ancients and, in addition, it fails to suggest the spider's poisonousness. Karl Marx's Spectre of Communism would be too gruesome an alternative even for the communists to live with willingly. At any rate, the subject of an international flag is not one to be taken other than seriously all around and, judging by its own effective emblems, the Soviet authorities are not without their successes in that field. Among other things, they have done their best to run off with the particularly stirring color of red.

In sum, relative to our legal partnership in the UN, communism violates the first and great Commandment, and consequently demoralizes the intent of the ways and means by which to obey the second part of the supreme law. Even the strongest people on earth must yearn sometimes for the right kind of encouragement and a hand that helps when needed. It is dangerous, as well as wrong, to do so through an atheistic organization, like the present "United Nations."

In the sequence of events, the general principle, good or evil, may not determine the character of each thought and deed considered separately. The worst kind of political organization can have some relatively good projects. But it is the integrating principle, chosen either deliberately or by default, that determines, nevertheless, the *trend* of the operation in the right, or wrong, direction.

The present UN, being as wrong at source as it is, will, perhaps, disappear automatically from the scene one of these days before too long, and without too much disturbance. But it would be a shining example of extremely wishful thinking now to take such a happy reorganization or demise for granted. Meanwhile, as always, in the human society of nations, it is right, in principle, if not always possible immediately, in practice, to seize the initiative as the way to establish, and then maintain, a supremacy under Divine Providence, a benevolent sovereignty in which each man learns why and how to help his neighbor to accomplish his stewardship in full.

And, to temper such an impersonal finding, there is a reason why that bears on all efforts of the nations and of lesser gatherings to work together for good. It can be expressed in many ways. Taking counsel, again, from a thought of France's Saint-Exupéry, it is the sight and knowledge of wasted talents that torments humanity. It is the feeling of talent wasted and of promise lost in the created image of the Maker of all things, the Judge of all men.

CHAPTER FOURTEEN

Patriotism, Readiness and Action

"It is the common fate of the indolent to see their rights become a prey to the active. The condition upon which God hath given liberty to man is eternal vigilence; which condition if he break, servitude is at once the consequence of his crime and the punishment of his guilt."

JOHN P. CURRAN
Speech upon the Right of
Election in Ireland, 1794.

I T is about time that we, among others, review the relationship that is supposed to exist between readiness and action, and think again about the importance of this relationship from the standpoint of patriotism.

A number of matters seem especially likely to be involved in such a project of review. For example, there is the subject of preparedness for favorable developments, as well as preparedness against ideas and events of the threatening kind. There is again the question of supremacy, and of why a nation, capable of overcoming an evil sovereignty, should stand by without taking action sufficient to free innocent victims of oppression.

There is, for instance, the process of the fulfillment of an idea that needs to be examined further, along with the phenomenon of the cycle in general. There are the political implications of the cyclical process.

Patriot, according to its derivation, is another word for "fellow countryman." A patriot is one who loves his country and does his best to safeguard her welfare. He is the unit of the democratic society and the possessor of the strengths with which the nation tries to fulfill her political and other ideals. Patriotism is, in fact, akin to religion. For a nation whose mottos are "In God We Trust" and "Do unto others as you would they should do unto you," the flag is like the emblem on the altar. The Stars and Stripes of the United States is a symbol of the eternal principle, no less than is the cross of the church. For the United States, the Bible and American history are essentials of education.

Christian civilization is characterized by a willing delegation of authority and corresponding responsibility by one patriot to another. It is also marked by a voluntary division of the work to be done by, and among, the various members of the community. The delegation and the division are of the kind that depend upon mutual confidence among men. Patriotic Christianity leads men willingly to fulfill the promise of their being, through the exercise of sovereign power within a cycle governed by the two Great Commandments.

"Ready, willing and able"—these watchwords of the United States Marine Corps, like the Marine Corps itself, have a special quality of greatness that we can be truly thankful to have in our midst. In its search for fundamentals this book soon found that the ideals represented by these words were needed as integral parts of any course of reasoning, such as the present argument.

In the preceding chapters, we have considered some of the essentials of ability and willingness. It is willingness, or, more precisely, the human ability to decide intentionally, that brings readiness and action alive and that gives moral significance to both of them.

In the context of human events, it is sometimes difficult enough, if not practically impossible, to tell where readiness ends and action begins, or where action ends and readiness for further action begins to take form. There are various reasons for this fact. Some of the reasons are so obvious that we seldom consider them.

One of the various reasons is that readiness and action are not only interdependent elements of a system, but are also different phases in the actual operation of the system. They are different aspects of a given process. One phase of the whole cycle of events tends to shade imperceptibly into another phase.

And that fact points to another reason, which we should go into more carefully a little later on. It is that any number of ideas, great and less than great, are trying to fulfill their respective cycles at one and the same time in the course of events.

Readiness means being prepared for what one is about to do. To be ready is to be equipped or supplied with what is needed for *immediate* action. Readiness can be in terms of the physical, or of the spiritual, or of both. It is into readiness on the moral plane, where elements of the spiritual and the physical naturally work together, that we need most to inquire at present.

An act is either a doing or a thing done in the sense of a deed, including, among other deeds, the spoken and the written word. An action implies that a cycle is still in progress, rather than implying motion in the detached sense of anything which is not at rest.

Action can be considered as strictly mechanical, as chemical or as of other physical form, or it can be thought of as involving human effort. As also in the case of readiness, we are mainly concerned, at present, with action as related to the requirements of a moral issue.

2.

The worst thing that can happen to an army is to be caught unprepared. That, at least, is what the U. S. Army Air Corps used to teach at Harrisburg. But our findings in this book indicate that there is something even worse than that, not only for an army but also for any embattled patriot. It is to be caught prepared.

It is questionable, of course, that anyone fully prepared in every way could be caught off guard. Nevertheless, to stand by with adequate means to seize the initiative, and still to be caught hands down is going about as far as anyone can go to invite disaster. Why?

The moral issue, in general, is to recognize and overcome evil in the community at first sign, to keep continually the upper hand of evil in each and every respect, as of here and now. Existence as a simple matter of self-preservation can not afford to let evilly-inclined forces gain an ascendancy. It is this fact, among others, that illustrates the force which naturally transforms readiness into action in the prototype of perfection.

The ideal calls for readiness and action to be as one, for action and reaction to be immediate, for all of the forces that enter into an event to be balanced always among themselves in such manner as to be inclined continually in the right direction. Nietzsche must have sensed this fact when he philosophized gloomily about what happens to anyone who is forced to remain continually on his guard. Lord Byron stated

the case in more positive fashion and with more enthusiasm—
"Know ye not, who would be free themselves must strike the
first blow."

Since the different and ever-changing hazards of the cal-
culated risk are practically beyond number, a general rule
seems to be required. After all, people grow strong not by
overcoming obstacles any old way, but by overcoming obstacles rightly.

The usually small detail can become, for the moment, of
immense importance but, as a rule politically for instance, it
is best to concentrate attention on those factors in a situation
which, by reference to guiding principle, rank high in an
order of first things first. It is better as a rule to pay attention
to those factors in a situation which are of a determining importance and influence—factors such as the maintaining of a
benevolent supremacy and of educating the youth accordingly—and, in the resulting trend, to let secondary or dependent factors take care of themselves under due supervision at
various levels of responsibility and authority.

In the human community, there is always a potential of
improvement, in that mankind, in terms of space and time, can
only approach and not entirely reach perfection. There is always a difference in level between the perfect ideal and the
actual state of affairs. There is always something further that
is worth while striving for in order to make life complete.

Our forebears, the Founding Fathers of these United States,
did not wait for events to work themselves out in one way
or another. Patience is no more a means and an end in itself
than is perseverence. The nature of the purpose beyond the
abstract virtue itself is the determining element. Our early
patriots chose to pursue their ideals, even if it meant the sacrifice of their lives on earth. In a dynamic system, such as the
system of Christian morality and its political counterpart,

errors of omission are to be avoided even more than errors of commission.

Action that is right originates in good thought. It is in the well-chosen idea or in the mistaken ideal, as the case may be, that we are to find the reason for a nation's strength and ready willingness in the patriotic mission—or, else, to find the reason for a nation's confusion, weakness and procrastination.

How is it that a supposedly Christian nation like our own, ready and able as it is physically, can be unwilling, not to say sometimes paralyzed, when it comes to taking effective action against the mounting tide of political atheism? It is because the ideals and the ideas of the members of our community, as a nation, have become confused in terms of supreme principle. The standards by which to judge right and wrong action have become obscured, neglected or discarded.

The world now is not in an ordinary contest of arms. The conflict is, first and last, between supreme beliefs. And that leaves much to be accounted for in the intervening cycle.

There is again, for example, the matter of timing. Time, in itself, is an abstraction. As such, it works for or against no one in particular. But time, as a factor of the daily event, is linked concretely to change and to progress. It goes without saying, except as a notation for the record, that the final purpose of any mission in the world has to be accomplished step by step, in keeping with relative abilities, capabilities and other circumstances, as of a given place and moment within the cycle of achievement.

In the armed conflict, or in a comparable test of the kind, potentially decisive weapons may lose their actual value, either if they be used at too early a stage in their development and availability, or if they be withheld from their intended use so long as to have become obsolescent.

The United States should not rush to start a war, world-wide or other, but the contrary. That fact is not taken to be at issue. Rather, it is a matter of gaining the initiative and of bringing continual and well-tempered pressures to bear on the evil opponent, in spite of the risk of war—a risk which exists anyhow and which, in principle, and accordingly in practice, is lessened, not increased, by moral courage and righteous action as well as by readiness.

3.

The political platform is, in general, a good idea and a useful institution. On the moral plane of thought, the planks of the platform represent the explicit grounds on which a group of persons chooses to stand together for purposes which are taken to be primarily political. Moreover, the concept of a platform fits in nicely with the idea that the world is flat, a useful idea within its limitations.

But the system of government discernible from the workings of human nature, the system in regard to which these pages endeavor to advance a theory, includes more than a number of good planks. It includes more than a number of good, but perhaps conflicting, objectives lined up and nailed down, side by side, for more or less chance reasons of expediency.

While we have been viewing the Aztecs with surprise and turning up our noses at the Incas for not having discovered the physical principle of the wheel, have we not been thoughtless enough ourselves? Have we, ourselves, not been unimaginative enough to have overlooked politically the spiritual principle of the moral cycle of fulfillment?

Abstract ideals, separately and together, naturally try to fulfill themselves by means of cycles involving concrete aims, and ways and means. The force of an idea tries to fulfill itself by action, even if the action to begin with be but a spoken word.

The various essentials of an order of fulfillment are designed, according to the master plan of nature viewed in prototype, to work willingly and successfully together toward the achievement of a rightly desired aim. For an actual system to bring other results is a signal that something is wrong. A benevolent sovereignty, being a supremacy of good will, pictures kindred ideas, each so well balanced in actual practice as to be able to accomplish the cycle of its particular aim, with means left over in the process by which to help others in the common cause.

If the circle in the abstract be taken as the symbol of perfection, as has frequently been the case from time immemorial, then a cycle, in terms of motion, may well be taken as the circle's dynamic counterpart.

The cycle is characteristic of the workings of nature. This fact is noticeable, not only on the plane of the physical considered separately, but also on the moral plane of the everyday event. The passive and the active, the potential and the kinetic, the abstract and the concrete, the thought, the word and the deed, are but qualitative differences among the elements which enter systematically into the cycle of fulfillment of the chosen aim. They are among the elements which are discernible in the system of human existence itself.

A cycle may be defined in general terms as a "complete course of operations of some kind, returning into itself and restoring the original." This definition is certainly vague enough to leave plenty to the imagination. To point it up, we might observe a few examples, keeping in mind the while the pertinent question of why patriotic readiness, for instance, does not always lead to as prompt action as it should.

In terms of thermo-dynamics—and again, if indirectly, by

courtesy of Count Rumford—a cycle is a series of operations at the end of which the working substance is returned to its original state, ordinarily with an accompanying conversion of heat into mechanical work, or vice versa.

Science, for further example, has uncovered the now well-supported fact that celestial bodies move cyclically in relation to one another. According to astronomers of today, our solar system is a tiny part of the immense Milky Way, some parts of which we can see with our own eyes by gazing into the heavens on a clear and starry night.

The Milky Way is, so to speak, a system in which inter-related particles of matter and other forms of physical energy function under natural law. The system comprises billions of stars, some of which are apparently millions of times larger than our sun.

Equilibrium within equilibrium, cycle upon cycle, star drawn toward star, the physical system of the universe moves swiftly through space, from moment to moment, toward the fulfillment of a cosmic purpose still beyond the comprehension of man on the Earth. Meanwhile, in the un-finished cycle, an equilibrium among moving forces inclines in one direction or the other, and we are brought again to an oft considered assumption—it is only in a state of per-fection that being, in itself, is both a means and an end.

Then, there is also the illustration of the worldly cycle of life of the many species of plant and of animal. There is the cycle of human thought and act which, observable in part, now interests us most of all—and which encourages us no little because the innate faculty of human choice enables conscientious effort.

Among the more intriguing phenomena there is the subject matter of the vortex theory in hydrodynamics, a theory akin, in turn, to the vortex-atom theory. In a perfect fluid, the vortex theory reasons, a portion of fluids the particles of which have rotary motion—i.e. a vortex, in case anyone has forgotten —could not be formed by mechanical means. But, if such a vortex existed, it would be indestructible, whatever change of shape it might pass through.

Domestic and foreign aims within a national policy. Ideas working well together or, on the contrary, in opposition one to another. Good ideas fulfilling themselves, in spite of opposition, by means of deeds of essentially the same character as that of the good ideas themselves.

A cycle of human achievement is not necessarily one only of rise and fall. Again there is the matter of trend. The economic law of so-called diminishing returns is seen to apply always in affairs predominantly physical, but physical reality is relative, not absolute. Man can imagine an ideal that guides toward increasingly productive cycles of abundance; in the light of a truly reasonable perfection, such an ideal, not its opposite, makes sense.

According to our theory of benevolent supremacy, human existence operates in a definite cycle of fulfillment, not in some relatively vague and endless line of development. The uncertainties of fulfillment stem from man's ignorance, coupled with his faculty of choice or free will. And every man-made system that fails to have a purpose above and beyond itself is suspect, if not already doomed. In respect to purpose, there is the further implication that the same would be true of the universe itself.

At man's everyday level of observation, the sequence of human events may appear to trail off endlessly into space and time, even as the earth may seem to be flat and always stationary. If human existence trails off aimlessly and does not operate in a cycle of achievement, however, it is the only comparable system around us that, by nature—or in principle —does not imply the cycle of fulfillment.

What this amounts to is that, apparently, a lot of us have been going around in cycles, not to say circles, without knowing it.

And according to the foregoing observations, plus a few relatively untested imaginings, it also turns out that the now famous equation $E = mc^2$, together with the strange cylindrical graph that represents the operational trend of physical energies in terms of Relativity's space-time continuum, is only a part, even though an important part, of reality.

Instead of talking about planes of thought, it might be more nearly the truth to speak of cycles of thought within coördinated systems. Instead of related planes of thought, physical, moral and spiritual, it might be better and more useful to discern interrelated cycles of thought.

It might be best of all to recognize one concept, or magnificent idea, which is capable of fulfilling itself—and does so—physically, morally and spiritually, at one and the same time in countless thousands of interrelated forms of excellence. Principles working within a principle; thoughts within a thought. One principle supreme. One great concept.

CHAPTER FIFTEEN

Peace

"If I must choose between righteousness and peace, I choose righteousness."

THEODORE ROOSEVELT
America and the World War

FOR some while I have been thinking that Antaeus should be brought into the present proceedings. It looks as if it would have to be now or never. This seems, moreover, to be the proper place to bring him in. He had a quality in common with righteousness.

Antaeus, you recall, was a mythological character who, according to an ancient record, was imagined originally by the Greeks. Of giant size, he was a wrestler and was long considered invincible. This was for an unusual reason. Leaving his father out of the story, his mother was a goddess, Gaea, the Earth. Every time Antaeus was thrown to the ground his strength was renewed, not primarily because it was the ground but because the Earth represented his origin. To be held aloft, out of touch with the immediate source of his might, led finally to his undoing.

It is the spiritual ideal that determines the character of righteousness and that finally sustains the fulfillment of the righteous cause. But when righteousness becomes, or tries to become, detached from the Earth, it neglects its element of human choice and fallibility. It can turn into bigotry or self-satisfaction, and into fixed ideas that lead even to tyranny.

It takes a continual touch of physical, as well as spiritual, reality for righteousness to be able to perform its appointed rôle. Even as an abstract quality, it can not afford to mistake itself for absolute goodness. It has to do specifically with the moral issue. Righteousness is not the final aim, it is the way toward the final ideal of perfection, and the way toward any true ideal, be it comparatively simple like a single virtue, or complex like the political ideal of peace.

As an ideal, peace can be thought of abstractly as a perfectly balanced state of affairs. It can also be thought of as a quality in the sense of tranquility. But the political ideal of "peace" needs also to be considered as a concrete fact, not as an abstract condition of affairs capable, in itself, of being both a means and an end. For it is not the kind of idea nor the kind of ideal that is self-sustaining morally.

At the beginning, it is also to be observed that peace is not simply a vague standard that can be approached, if not fully attained. Peace is, in fact, a collective ideal. It is made up of many individual thoughts, the actual fulfillment of which is, by nature, systematic. To shout about peace is not to have peace automatically. The effective cycle of the peaceful ideal includes various ideas and acts and standards of perfection that go well together, and that are chosen accordingly.

The supreme principle, as evidenced to the mind in the two Great Commandments of the Christian faith, is the integrating force that gives to every relative aim and cycle, in particular, a purpose beyond and above itself, and so determines the right direction. It is in the everlastingly good trend that there is no such thing as the "impossible." And there are comparable or analogous ways and means of approaching the true perfection in every area of human concern and endeavor.

Not long ago the National Broadcasting Company Symphony gave a concert in New York City's Carnegie Hall. This is the same symphony orchestra of which the famed maestro, Arturo Toscanini, had been for so long the conductor and the genius.

At the recent concert now in mind, Signor Toscanini having retired from the active field of his profession because of his advancing years, the members of the orchestra, each so well versed and so well skilled in his art, continued, as in the past, to play the score practically to perfection. Without a conductor on the podium, they together played their respective portions directly and voluntarily, in accord with the will of the composer.

It was an exceptional and high accomplishment that calls attention to a pattern of coöperation and a standard of perfection to be sought in other fields. On the other hand, but for the vivid recollection of Maestro Toscanini himself, would there not have been some quality, or element, lacking, something familiar and dear to the heart? The abstract ideal is an inevitable factor in the living of a human life, but the everyday design calls for a leader to personify the ideal. That was one of our observations long ago. As a dependable rule, the design calls for a leader to give human personality to the quality of the composition and a human touch today to the execution of the will of the composer in regard to the actual performance.

The achievement of the National Broadcasting Company symphony orchestra in the undertaking above mentioned has been more successful, for example, than the attainment of the classless society called for by the *Communist Manifesto* could, by its nature, ever be. Leadership, and, in particular, international leadership again, is a problem not to be overlooked in our remaining pages.

2.

Exactly what do most Americans have in mind when they think and talk about peace? Does the American distinguish carefully between the ideal and the aims of peace, on the one hand, and, on the other, the ways and means of achieving the aims and approaching the ideal? In all the world there have seldom been more important questions, and they are not new. The answers are for each and every citizen to choose for himself.

It is not always easy to view the underlying meaning of peace. It seems that we are more likely to think habitually of peace as an official absence of war. We are likely, at first, to imagine a formal reconciliation between former enemies, a reconciliation that ushers in an all-around condition of tranquility and happiness which is supposed to be almost self-sustaining, without more personal ado of an unpleasant kind. That is one way of defining peace, but it is not a good enough way. The issues that determine peace and war are substantive causes. They go deeper than a legal fiction. Witness Korea, where there was much bloodshed and plenty of confusion as between morality and geography, but no official declaration of war between the opposing forces.

After V-E Day and V-J Day of World War II, the Reds wanted Europe and Asia left to the mercies of communist ideology, so to speak, or left to soviet socialist propaganda supported by a fear of the Kremlin's growing military might unopposed.

One of the most effective slogans of Soviet Russia at that time was "The war is over, bring the boys home." It was an appealing slogan that helped immensely to advance the Soviet aim of causing a major disintegration of the Armed Forces of the Allies. A well-conceived demobilization is one thing. A hurried separation of millions of men from the service under emotional pressures is another.

If, in general, there be one word by which to mesmerize these United States of America in the 20th century up until now, it is the word peace, together with war as an opposite idea. Peace and war, in the abstract. Good and evil, in the abstract. But, concretely, what about right and wrong?

Our government is apparently so confused on the above subject these days that we have abandoned even the name "War Department." We now have, instead, the name "Department of Defense," as if it had become wrong to seize the initiative in the righteous cause! Who or whom do we think we are kidding, if not ourselves?

The title chosen at first for our present chapter was "Pax Americana." That was some years ago. Surely an American peace is not one under which tens of millions of people in the world are written off indefinitely to State slavery and left behind Red barriers, almost if not entirely unaided by the United States. Not forgetting the benefits that often can accrue from personal deliberation and discussion, or from official consultation, national and international, it is still true also that continual debate can be self-defeating, if not controlled by a purpose really greater than a well-intentioned routine.

Surely a nation does not lend its name to a peace in which it does not exert every force of which it is capable to free its own nationals unjustly held captive behind the so-called Iron Curtain. There are such captives now being used as pawns by the avowed enemies of every person and every nation believing in God.

Within present terms of reference, pacifism is taken to mean an official policy of avoiding a formal declaration of war on evil forces, political or other, at practically any price —morality to the contrary of such avoidance notwithstanding. The philosophy of pacifism forgets that there can be no absolute peace on earth, much less peace between opposite concepts of principle, each of which depends, for its fulfillment, on being supreme. But, for one reason, or another, and none of them righteous according to our findings, the Government of the United States gives many an indication that it has become unrealistic, not to say positivistic, in its approach to moral issues, both at home and abroad, pacifist rather than prudent in its approach to the Gordian knot of Soviet conquest and enslavement.

It is a fact that raises the fundamental question of the changelessness of natural ideal under the stress of circumstance. Does the discovery and the use of atomic power change the principle of human life? Does it change the scheme and pattern of the system in which opposition to progress in the right direction needs continually to be overcome? Do circumstances of place and time alter the great concept of perfection in which benevolence is supreme in every way, the concept which our theory has taken to be the ideal condition of thought itself?

The argument advanced during our inquiry gives an answer that is the same to each of the three questions. The answer is no—and, in the same breath, it is necessary to add that today's "Atomic Age" requires the highest degree of prudence in order for benevolent forces to regain and keep the upper hand once and for all. Prudence is required, well mixed with justice, fortitude and temperance, and also with faith, hope and charity.

We are likely to consider prudence a passive virtue only, but the opposite is true. It is often, although not always, prudent to act rather than to stand still. It can be recklessly imprudent to indulge in pacifism instead of taking the best action possible to seize the initiative, the best action possible under the circumstances, as viewed and decided upon in the light of knowledge, wisdom and the supreme ideal. Prudence is the matching of capabilities, and of strengths in being, against the forces of the opposition to be overcome.

That the present argument takes no stock in pacifism does not mean, however, that it leans toward militarism. On the contrary, it would be wrong indeed if the spirit and the policy of our government were to abandon the virtue of being temperate and were to swing, for no good reason, from one extreme of any kind to the other extreme. The argument of this book is for every peaceful step. It is against every warlike measure, except as it be necessary to the maintaining of due law and order. A nation's justification for going to war —call it war, or a police action, or by other name—is found, not in war itself, but in fighting for the benevolent ideals that finally distinguish man from brute.

In regard to the status of armed might, as also in regard to other instruments of power, those civilian in character, for example, it is the happy medium that is needed from moment to moment—the happy medium this time in the well-tempered sense of moderation. Due moderation, dynamically, is the amount of force of one kind and another that is necessary, as of here and now, to overcome opposition to progress in the right direction. In addition, prudence suggests that enough force, military and other, is needed to form a reserve against emergencies in the trend of the foreseeable future. This definition, as it should, leaves the interpretation of adequate and other such general terms to a current exercise of human choice. Pacifism and militarism do not spring from set figures nor even from enacted law.

Neither is peace of a nature to be legislated. The important function of the honorable agreement among two, or more, members of mankind is not one to belittle. Clear agreements in good faith can help to avoid misunderstandings and can act as deterrents to undue conflict, open or concealed. But peace among men can not be secured by legislative action, any more than true worshipfulness and charity can be made secure by such means. For a law really to be effective and to build for good, the spirit must support the law and the truth must support the spirit.

Peace is of the mind. Peace of mind depends on a knowledge and practice of the truth about human existence, according to the working design of life which we can discern. The individual persons, who together make up a community, must have peace of mind, before there can be real peace within the community, be it a nation, or the community of nations. In an order of first things first—and granting the paramount importance of a benevolent supremacy in which the spiritual and the physical are joined systematically in the moral realm—education in the whole truth, not legislation, nor government fiat, takes precedence as the way to bring peace ever closer to the world.

There can be no just nor lasting peace within a nation where citizen is turned against citizen through education in falsehood, or through ill-balanced ideals and ill-inclined policies and practices of government that amount to unequal treatment before the law. There can be no real peace achieved by our nation, or by any other, through pacifism in the face of legislative inroads upon the freedom of the individual, within the framework of his inborn rights and duties toward his fellow countrymen and toward his fellow man elsewhere.

Peace within the nation does not come from the injustice and the precarious balance of a public debt that throws, or tries to throw, an overwhelming obligation of the past and

present upon a blameless future. Along with the overpower-
ing of other threats and acts against good government, at
home and from abroad, chronic indebtedness must be elimi-
nated, if there is to be a just and lasting peace. A leader among
nations does not spend time and resources hacking at the
branches, while the affairs of one ally after another trend into
serious political, economic and other difficulties. The leader
attacks promptly at the roots that grow iron curtains and
public debts.

Progress toward peace does not come from tax laws that
intend to make the individual materially dependent on the
would-be totalitarian State, and that, in the process, tend
to injure individual enterprise in the fulfillment of a personal stewardship. The 16th Amendment to the United States
Constitution, the 16th Amendent as an instrument for the
confiscation of private property, has to be curbed for the
good of everyone, believe it, or not.

Above all, the cause of peace is not advanced, but the contrary, by a political philosophy of atheism, nor is it aided by
a confusion of self-righteousness with righteousness itself. It
is advanced by a philosophy that is centered on a responsible
as well as an all-powerful Creator.

Within the present political parties of the United States,
there are citizens who stand forth, individually, as initiators
and staunch supporters of good aims and corresponding action.
In both of our major political parties today, there are to be
found citizens of highest character and excellent ability who
are capable of providing leadership in addition to effective
coöperation.

But the truly benevolent elements of the community are
too often divided among themselves by party names and
force of habit instead of by clear-cut political issues. They
lack a final rallying point in common, by which to make sure

that high policies of state are of a kind to strengthen instead of to defeat one another. Within the body politic they do not have the systematic support of an organization that never ceases to extend its influence to all areas of important interest, because it is guided by clearly unified, as well as the best of, ideals.

In the give and take of the daily life of a community, there are innumerable differences of opinion that can be, and rightly should be, reconciled peacefully, which is also to say reconciled without sacrifice of integrity and honor. In situations that involve primarily practice and procedure, in secondary considerations of one kind and another, there are numberless conflicts of interest in actual affairs that can be arbitrated morally.

On the other hand, there are a few, but overruling, matters of highest principle in which there can be no moral compromise at all. There is a dividing line to be drawn. There are conditions under which agreement, for agreement's sake, is not only wrong but also more than dangerous to the present and the future of a nation and of the people who make up the nation.

The dividing line again concerns the freedom of the individual to fulfill his stewardship in life in keeping with the supreme law of human nature which gives authority and responsibility to people, jointly and severally, the law of nature which seems often to be as one with the laws of thought and of existence.

In our present inquiry, we have tried to consider carefully the subject of unity as between religious and political truths. The facts observed lead to a conclusion that it is a subject of utmost import and consequence.

In the honor system of personal trustworthiness, which the majority of the people of our country speak of as Christian civilization, the need becomes evident for a Church militant, as well as for a State militant, in decisions that are above and beyond moral compromise. Good will in the Government, as in the school, can ill afford to be without the intentional support of the pulpit. The flag unfurled in the good cause needs to be recognized as an emblem of an eternal as well as of a temporal sovereignty.

Indeed, history gives many indications that, lacking the church militant—militant righteously—a nation's decline is but a question of time.

And, within the same terms of reference, there is another fact to be recorded. If any member of a body politic doubts that religious truths, as compared with political and other kinds of verity, are the more difficult of scientific proof, it can be food for his thoughts that his opinion has been arrived at by means of thinking and that today, scientifically, there is not yet a theory acknowledged as proven in regard to the nature of thought itself. It would seem that, in the systematic pattern of reality, all truths of any kind are designed to be accepted originally on faith.

Our country needs a national party whose members are dedicated explicitly, one and all, not to compromises contrary to morality, but to a whole policy of doing and, thereby, of proving again what is right in the real and best sense of the word.

3.

After two World Wars, the winners of the battles have failed to turn victory into a lasting peace among the nations.

A few years ago, and for the first time in recorded history, a people and their government—the American people and the Government of the United States—had the means at their disposal to gain a physical ascendancy, not to say a complete supremacy in physical might, throughout the whole of the globe. At the same time, they had the means, also, to draw a sustaining strength from a guiding principle which could, and still can, bring about a benevolent rule in political affairs, near and far. They had not come intentionally and willingly, however, into the responsibility of world power. Greatness as a nation among nations had been, not only entrusted to them, but also "thrust upon them" in no small degree.

They have recognized their responsibility in some ways but not in others. Integration, when and if any, in matters of high policy, has not been adequate. The authority was not grasped firmly and, in spite of good intentions, has not been exerted effectively, either within the nation, or in international affairs. On the contrary, it has been in the process of being lost, due, on the surface, to misplaced confidence in promises of the communists, or, to be more exact, mostly in promises and assurances of the communist rulers of the Union of Soviet Socialist Republics.

But, in reality, it is finally impossible to separate domestic and foreign issues. A nation's strengths and weaknesses begin and end at home. A deliberate desire to assume the right and duties of leadership is necessary. Otherwise, according to the observable nature of human events, the leadership is sure to pass to some other people and government willing and happy to have it. Lacking a benevolent victor from out the armed conflict, lacking a willing victor who is hopeful, yet watchful of the hard-won supremacy, every hour, every day, from year to year, from century to century, there is little more than a precarious armistice internationally.

In principle, and in actual fact, however, it is not too late today to make amends in the reasonably foreseeable future. The responsibility remains as pressing as ever. The authority is still within grasp. The good qualities, the good will and the many accomplishments of the American people go without saying in the present pages. The mistakes of policy can not be undone, but a measure of compensation is possible. It is possible, for instance, to regain the initiative through well-chosen and mutually strengthening aims and acts, and through continually good leadership, from here on in.

Ideally, nations welcome the coöperation of strong, right arms, if joined with good ideas, at any place and time on earth. Besides the wish for mutual protection against an enemy, there can be the more enduring bond among allies that comes from a supreme principle held in common, a tie that stems from changeless ideals and from similar ideas about putting principle and ideals to work in the community. It has to be kept in mind, nevertheless, that, subject to the due exception to the rule, allies, in the form of other bodies politic, are not always a force to be relied upon. The hope of immediate reward and the fear of immediate punishment are conditions that are as tempting, politically, as they are in other ways.

The good cause is the restless search for a perfection of which peace is the star and righteousness the guide. It is a cause in which mankind is allied by nature and in which a nation never finds itself without immense support, potential, if not already actually in force. But, as a last question, what of effective leadership in the good cause, in one that is a cause in common, yet torn by current disagreements which confuse the paramount issue between right and wrong, and between good and evil?

Two facts, among others bearing on the subject, are relevant and point to the answer to the question.

One is that there is no real leadership without a corresponding duty and responsibility actually to lead, not to side-